Cocaine and Crack

Marilyn Carroll

—The Drug Library—

ENSLOW PUBLISHERS, INC.

Bloy St. and Ramsey Ave.   P.O. Box 38
Box 777   Aldershot
Hillside, NJ 07205   Hants GU12 6BP
U.S.A.   U.K.

Library of Congress Cataloging-in-Publication Data

Carroll, Marilyn.
    Cocaine and crack/Marilyn, Carroll.
        p. cm. — (The Drug Library)
    Includes biographical references and index.
    ISBN 0-89490-472-8
    1. Cocaine habit—Juvenile literature. 2. Crack (Drug)—
Juvenile literature. [1. Cocaine habit. 2. Crack (Drug) 3. Drug Abuse.]
    I. Title. II. Series.
RC568.C6C37 1994
616.86'47—dc20   93-43451
                                                        CIP
                                                        AC

Printed in the United States of America.

10 9 8 7 6 5 4 3 2 1

Illustration Credits: Adapted from Coca Exotica, Joseph Kennedy, Associated
University Presses, Inc.: Cranbury, NJ, 1985, p. 7; Drug Abuse Warning Network
(DAWN), Advance Report Number 4, September, 1993, U.S. Department of
Health and Human Services, Public Health Service, p. 59; Journal of American
Medical Association, Vol. 263, No. 24, June 27, 1990, p. 42; Marilyn Carroll, pp.
25, 30, 32; Medicinal Plants, Robert Bentley and Henry Trimen, J.A. Churchill:
London, 1880, from the collection of the Wangensteen Historical Library,
University of Minnesota, p. 14; Monitoring the Future Survey, U.S. Department
of Health and Human Services, p. 63; National Families in Action Survey, 1993,
pp. 77, 86.

Cover Illustration: Drug Enforcement Administration

Contents

1

The History of Cocaine Use and Abuse

How Long Has Cocaine Been Used?

Cocaine, which comes from the coca plant, was probably used thousands of years ago, long before recorded history. Drawings showing its use were found on pottery in northwestern South America dating back from 1100 to 1500 A.D.[1] At the peak of the Incan civilization, Peruvian Indians grew coca plants containing cocaine to be used mainly by the ruling class. It was thought that coca was a gift from the gods. When the Spanish Conquistadors arrived in South America the religious use of coca began to taper off.[2] At first the Spaniards thought coca was sinful and tried to stop its use. They later found that if they allowed their Indian slaves to use it they worked harder, and the use of coca began to increase. Coca became such a valued product it was

traded as money. The Spaniards paid Incan workers in coca leaves for mining and hauling gold and silver.

In What Ways Has Cocaine Been Used Throughout History?

For a long period of time cocaine was used by chewing coca leaves. When you chew cocaine leaves, the effects last one to two hours. Indians from South America pack the leaves into their cheeks and gradually swallow the juices from them throughout the day. Often lime or ash is added to the coca leaves. This results in better absorption of the drug into the cheek and a stronger drug effect. Indians use the leaves to feel less tired and less hungry.[3] It helps them work longer and harder.[4]

During the last half of the 19th century, Europeans became interested in the coca leaf, and its active chemical, cocaine. Cocaine was separated from the coca leaf in 1860 by Albert Niemann. There are several examples of how European interest helped to promote the spread of cocaine. Angelo Mariani was a French chemist who imported tons of coca leaves from Peru. He used extracts from the coca leaf in many products such as tea and cough drops. His coca leaf wine was called *Vin Mariani*, and it made him famous. People believed that the wine strengthened, refreshed, and restored the spirit. Mariani wine was used by well-known individuals such as President William McKinley, Pope Leo XVIII and the Czar of Russia (Nicholas II). The Pope was so impressed with this wine that he awarded Angelo Mariani with a gold medal.[5]

Dr. William S. Halsted was one of the founders of The Johns Hopkins University School of Medicine and was considered the father of modern surgery. He also influenced the

6

This 1893 advertisement for Vin Mariani was probably a significant factor in its popularity among the people of that time.

7

way cocaine was used. In the 1880s, he used purified cocaine and the newly developed hypodermic needle to inject cocaine under the skin to numb surface areas. He also injected cocaine deeper near a nerve to block pain and other sensations in a large area of the body. Cocaine worked well as an anesthetic for surgery. Halsted used cocaine on himself and eventually became addicted. He suffered mental illness from this addiction. His physician friends sent him away on an extended cruise, but that did not have lasting results. Eventually, lifelong addiction to morphine replaced his addiction to cocaine.[6]

Another famous physician who worked with cocaine was Sigmund Freud. In 1884 Freud was a young ambitious physician in Vienna, Austria. He tried to make a name for himself by trying cocaine on patients with heart disease, nervous exhaustion, and morphine withdrawal. He was particularly interested in helping a friend who had become dependent on morphine. Freud was so impressed with the results that he published a paper entitled "On Coca". This paper reviewed the history of cocaine and praised the drug's ability to treat several medical conditions.[7]

At about the same time Freud also worked with an eye surgeon to develop the use of cocaine as an anesthetic for eye surgery. Cocaine continued to be useful for this purpose for over one hundred years. However, its popularity for treatment of almost all other conditions rapidly declined. Shortly after Freud's friend began using cocaine regularly, he began to have serious side effects such as tremors and hallucinations (seeing or hearing things that are not there). Within three years after Freud became famous for introducing the medical use of cocaine, he was accused of being reckless and irresponsible.[8] Eventually, Freud admitted that cocaine had its limitations and he turned against the drug.[9] By 1891, there had been two hundred reports of intoxication and thirteen deaths, including one of Freud's patients.

Word spread about the dangers of cocaine use, but toward the end of the 1800s and early 1900s it continued to be used in patent medicines and home remedies. Cocaine was often included as a secret ingredient in medicines, but its stimulant effects were clearly advertised. One drug company, Parke-Davis, sold cocaine in about fifteen different products including cigarettes and a syringe and needle kit.[10]

In 1906 the Pure Food and Drug Act required cocaine to be listed as an ingredient in all patent medicines. Patent medicines were sold by individuals or drug companies to remedy many common illnesses. In 1914 the Harrison Narcotic Act prohibited the use of cocaine in medicines and other products. By this time cocaine use had become socially unacceptable, and it was associated with the lower class and criminals. No one was able to successfully fight to keep it legal when it was banned.

After the Harrison Act of 1914, cocaine was less available and much more expensive. There are few reports of cocaine related problems from 1914 through the 1960s. We have no good estimates of how much cocaine was used. There was some reported use of the drug by actors, actresses, and jazz musicians throughout the early 20th century.[11] There was a further decline in cocaine use during the 1930s when amphetamine (speed) became inexpensive and available. Amphetamine gained rapid popularity because it was inexpensive, effective for weight reduction, and believed to be safe and not addictive.

Famous People Using Cocaine

In addition to the famous physicians of the 1880s and some of the best known religious and political figures who drank Mariani wine, there were a number of other famous people who used cocaine. Among them were the author Jules Verne, who wrote *Twenty-Thousand Leagues under the Sea*, and the American inventor Thomas Edison. The author of Sherlock Holmes mysteries, Sir Arthur Conan Doyle, told how his character Sherlock Holmes injected cocaine into his veins.[12] This Doyle said was done to stimulate and clear Sherlock Holmes' mind when he became bored.

During the 1970s, cocaine reappeared among many famous people in sports and the entertainment business. Snorting cocaine became a fashionable practice. Since cocaine carried such a high price tag at that time, it was a sign of success for those who could afford to use it regularly. In the 1980s, comedian John Belushi died of a cocaine-heroin (speedball) overdose. Comedian Richard Pryor was badly burned from freebasing cocaine with ether.

In 1990 the mayor of Washington, D.C., Marion Barry, admitted using cocaine and several other drugs. He was forced to quit his job as mayor. Since treatment he has been active in community service. Many sports figures have received publicity for cocaine and other drug use. The increased awareness of drug use among athletes is due to urine testing that has become part of the rules of competition. All types of sports have been affected including boxing, soccer, basketball, football, and baseball. In the case of Len Bias, a basketball star, the results were fatal. Cocaine causes sudden death in some athletes because it produces cardiac arrhythmia, an irregular heartbeat. The heartbeat can remain irregular even during periods when cocaine is not being used. When the heart is stressed by intense physical exercise, it vibrates rapidly. This is called fibrillation. Sometimes fibrillation can be stopped and a normal heartbeat can be restored, but when it can not, it results in death.

In other cases of cocaine use, the athlete is suspended until a treatment program is completed. It is unfortunate that some of the role models for youth from the sports and entertainment world have become known as cocaine users. The positive side, however, is that after treatment they often work hard talking about why not to take drugs.

Questions for Discussion

1. Do you think that cocaine should be allowed for medical use?

2. What kind of problems does cocaine abuse cause in families?

3. How do we know if drugs like cocaine are added to our foods and beverages today?

2

What Does Cocaine Look Like?

Processing of Coca Leaves
Where Do They Come From?

Coca leaves come from western South America in countries such as Peru and Bolivia. They grow on a shrub called the coca plant (*Erythroxylan coca*). The plants grow best at high altitudes. The processing of cocaine begins with collecting the leaves and mixing them in a pit in the ground with gasoline or kerosene, sulfuric acid, and other chemicals. This separates the chemical cocaine from the watery, leafy material. This mixture is then filtered to remove most of the liquid, and the grayish mash is left to dry in the sun.[1] What is left is *coca paste* which consists of cocaine and some plant residue which has an unpleasant odor. In South America coca paste is mixed with tobacco and smoked. It is called "basuco"[2], and in South America there is increasing

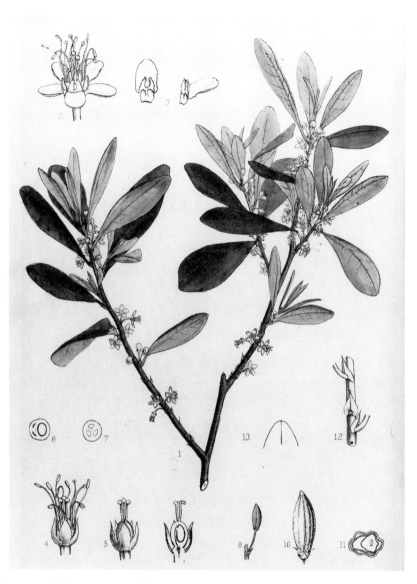

The many different parts of the coca plant are shown individually, surrounding the plant itself. While it may look like any other harmless plant, the effects of the coca plant can be deadly.

addiction and death from basuco. This form of cocaine is even more addictive and dangerous than crack. Its use has not been reported in the United States.

With further processing the coca paste can be made into *cocaine hydrochloride*, a white powder, which is the form used in the United States for intravenous injection and snorting. This form is pure cocaine plus salt. It takes about one hundred pounds of coca leaves to make one pound of cocaine hydrochloride.[3] Because of this, cocaine is processed in South America before it is smuggled into the United States.

Crack or *cocaine base* is made by further processing that removes the salt and leaves pure cocaine. In the early 1980s cocaine base or freebase was extracted with ether, a dangerous chemical that can catch on fire and explode. In the mid 1980s it was discovered that cocaine base or crack could be made by adding baking soda. After a sticky substance formed, it was washed with water, and the substance dried to form crack or "rock" cocaine. When this rock was heated, cocaine vapors could be inhaled.

Whether cocaine is used in the form of paste, cocaine hydrochloride, or crack, it is still the same chemical. Each of these substances consists of cocaine. Regardless of what form cocaine is in, it is the same drug and will affect the brain in the same way. The strength of cocaine's effect and the length of time that it lasts are determined by whether it is chewed (coca leaves), snorted (cocaine hydrochloride), injected intravenously (cocaine hydrochloride), or smoked (crack).[4] How it gets into the body determines how fast it gets to the brain, and how fast it gets to the brain determines what type of effect it will have.

How Does Cocaine Get Here?

Coca leaves are transported through Equador to Colombia in cars, trucks, buses, planes, or ships along the Western Coast of South America. Some cocaine is taken up the Amazon River on river boats. In Colombia, cocaine powder is manufactured in large cities such as Bogota or Medellin. From Colombia, cocaine is transported by plane to the East Coast cities of the United States, usually to Florida or New York. It is then transported to other cities. Recently cocaine has been arriving on direct flights to smaller cities. Some cocaine is also transported through Mexico to Texas and the West coast of the United States. There are many ways of hiding cocaine on commercial airline flights, in freight or mail compartments, or as personal baggage. There have even been cases of people swallowing balloons full of cocaine (body packers) to get them to the United States. Sometimes the balloons can burst before they completely passed through the person's digestive system, resulting in death. It was recently reported that cocaine can be hidden by including it in the manufacturing process for plastic items such as suitcases or bathtubs. When the materials are later dissolved, the cocaine can be recovered. Customs agents are able to inspect only about three out of every one hundred containers that arrive by ship or air.[5]

Colombia has been the number one supplier of cocaine to the United States during the last ten years. It is estimated that more than $500 billion is made in profit each year. About $12 billion of this revenue remains in the United States, much of it in South Florida. The rest of the billions of dollars are distributed in banks in the Cayman Islands, Panama, or other countries with bank secrecy laws.

16

There are several factors helping Colombia to make a big success out of selling cocaine.[6] First, the conversion of cocaine to carefully measured quantities of crack makes it easy to use. Second, the large supply makes it inexpensive. Third, in the United States drug dealers break some of the rules that were upheld by the previous drug lords. The drug trade is no longer kept within families or ethnic groups or in certain neighborhoods. Anyone can become a dealer or pusher. Sales to children which were forbidden ten or fifteen years ago are now permitted and encouraged. Finally, the mass marketing techniques have made crack widely available almost anywhere in the United States. This wide distribution makes it nearly impossible for Colombian law enforcement to control.

The monopoly of cocaine sales is an example of marketing genius. Cocaine reaches major cities like New York in large quantities called cells. It is then distributed to middlemen. They in turn distribute it to dealers. The dealer makes his money by selling the whole amount and adding on a charge for profit. He can also divide his supply into small amounts and add a profit to each. He can make more money by cutting the cocaine with lactose (milk sugar) and selling smaller amounts with a profit for each sale. This is called a pyramid organization. At the bottom are the pushers. The next level up is the dealers. Next in line are the distributors. The top of the pyramid consists of cartel members. Each member of the pyramid organization only deals with a few other members only one level up or down. No one member knows the whole chain of command. When there is an arrest or a bust it only involves a few members, and the organization continues to thrive. As you get higher in the pyramid structure, more money is made. If you get caught, there

is a longer prison term for those who are higher up in the organization.

Forms of Cocaine Currently In Use

Coca leaves are still chewed by native Peruvians and Bolivians. The effects of cocaine in this form last one or two hours. Coca leaves are not used in the United States because they are too bulky to smuggle in. Cocaine powder could also be taken orally. It would be absorbed more slowly than by smoking or snorting, but it would last longer. Taking cocaine by mouth has not been popular in this country. Coca tea can also be brewed from coca leaves. In South America coca tea is used at high altitudes to reduce the symptoms of altitude sickness such as fatigue, nausea, and dizziness.

Coca paste is also used in South America but rarely in the United States. The actual cocaine content in the remaining paste is quite high—greater than 50 percent. Coca paste is then dried and smoked in tobacco or marijuana cigarettes. Due to the solvents that are used in this process, coca paste often has an unpleasant taste and odor. Smoking coca paste is not common in the United States because its bulky form makes it difficult to ship and distribute. The added processing (to cocaine hydrochloride) makes the price higher and the profit larger for the South American cartels.

Cocaine hydrochloride, a white powder, is made from coca paste. There are other chemicals and waste products in the paste, and these are removed by adding a strong acid (hydrochloric acid). The remaining substance is then further purified by a washing and drying process. What remains is a white powder that contains cocaine and a salt. This form of cocaine is what is shipped to the United States from Colombia. It may then be diluted with sugars and cheaper drugs such as amphetamines. This form of cocaine is mixed with water and injected by some users. Other users place a "line" of the cocaine hydrochloride on a glass or mirror and snort it. In the 1980s it was popular to fill a small "measuring" spoon with cocaine for snorting. The 1991 National Household Drug Survey, conducted every year by the National Institute on Drug Abuse,[7] reported that 90 percent of those who have used cocaine have snorted it. About one-third of those surveyed reported injecting it and only one out of ten said they had smoked crack. These numbers count people who have used cocaine even once, so they include many of the people in the 1980s who briefly tried cocaine. Since crack was not available until the mid 1980s, not many people had used it by the time the survey was taken. These figures will probably change a lot when the next survey is taken because crack became very inexpensive and easy to use in the 1990s. A recent report indicates an increasing trend for youth to intravenously inject cocaine.[8]

Cocaine base. Another type of cocaine smoking is called freebasing. It began in the United States in the 1980s. For cocaine to burn or turn into small airborne particles, it is necessary to extract pure cocaine (base) from the salt, cocaine hydrochloride. The process used in the 1980s was called freebasing. It has since been replaced by a simpler safer method. The original process requires a lengthy chemical procedure that uses baking soda and other common chemicals to extract the cocaine base. It takes about ten grams of cocaine hydrochloride to make 8.5 grams of cocaine base. The base is then smoked in a water pipe or in tobacco or marijuana cigarettes. A dangerous

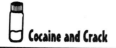

part of the freebasing process is the use of a highly flammable chemical called ether. If all of the ether does not evaporate before smoking, or if smoking takes place too close to the ether can, there could be an explosion and a fire.

Crack. In the mid 1980s a seemingly safer version of cocaine base became available on the streets. It was called crack. Crack can be made from the cocaine hydrochloride salt by adding baking soda and water. A similar process involving baking soda is used to make crack in crack houses. A solid, sticky mass is formed and is dried or boiled to become the rock or crystal that is sold on the street. Vapors from the rock can then be inhaled by putting the rock in a glass tube and heating it with a cigarette lighter.

Since crack appeared to be safer and was easier to use, it became very popular in the late 1980s. The demand and supply increased and the price decreased. In the mid 1980s, the price of a one-day supply, about a gram, of cocaine was around $100, making it an expensive habit. That is why it was mainly used by professionals or celebrities. In the late 1980s the price of crack dropped to approximately $10 per hit in the inner cities. The low price, easy storage, and ease of use have contributed to the growing abuse of crack through the 1990s.[9] Crack is nearly 100 percent pure. Crack does not mix well with water, although it does dissolve well in alcohol. Therefore cocaine base cannot be mixed with water or a salt water solution to be injected. Crack is also not usually taken orally. It is mainly used for smoking.

What Are the Medical Uses of Cocaine?

Cocaine has been used for medical reasons for hundreds of years. Although it was used by the Incas for centuries for religious and medical purposes,[10] its medical uses became most well-known in the latter 1800s.[11] In 1860 Albert Niemann extracted the active chemical from coca and named it cocaine. In 1879 Van Anrep used it to numb the tongue and the skin for surgical procedures. A few years later, in 1884, Carl Koller found that cocaine was very useful for eye surgery, and others such as Halsted, Corning, and Quince used cocaine for spinal anesthesia. This allowed the surgeon to numb larger parts of the body for more serious operations. In the early 1900s, drugs that were similar to cocaine like novocain (procaine) and xylacaine were developed in the laboratory. They replaced the more toxic cocaine.

There are currently very few medical uses for cocaine.[12] At one time it was used for eye surgery or to numb the eye during testing for glaucoma. It was found to cause ulcers on the cornea and to cloud vision. It is still used for surgery in the nose, throat, larynx, and lower respiratory system. Cocaine is ideal for surgery in these areas because its two major effects are anesthesia (numbing of sensation) and reducing the flow of blood. The ear, nose, and throat areas have a lot of blood vessels, and it helps to use a drug that minimizes bleeding. Since swallowing blood results in vomiting, reducing bleeding will lessen the strain on the nose and throat area after surgery. Less bleeding also allows the surgeons to see better. It has become more difficult, however, for ear, nose, and throat surgeons to use cocaine because of the licensing restrictions and high costs. They are substituting combinations of other drugs that have the same effects.

Cocaine was briefly used for another medical purpose in the 1970s. It was used with a combination of other drugs (methadone and alcohol) to treat the pain in people who were dying of cancer.[13] This mixture was called Brompton's mixture.[14]

An opioid drug like morphine or methadone relieves pain, but it puts the person in a clouded state. They may fall asleep frequently and be difficult to communicate with. When cocaine was added, it seemed to make patients more alert and it also helped relieve the pain. Cocaine is no longer being used for this purpose, however, because more effective pain medications have been developed for use with cancer patients.

Questions for Discussion

1. Do you think crack is a stronger drug than cocaine? Why/Why not?

2. How could we stop cocaine from getting into the United States?

3. Is cocaine like amphetamine (speed)?

3

What Are the Effects of Cocaine?

How Does Cocaine Affect Feelings and Moods?

The first time cocaine is used it may make the heart beat faster leading to a feeling of excitement and fear. This is followed by a sensation of well-being called euphoria.[1] These feelings will start within seconds if cocaine is injected or smoked, and this is called a rush. Shortly after cocaine is taken, users may also feel more sociable. They may also feel more energetic and will generally have good feelings about themselves. They may have increased sensation when their skin is touched and increased desire for contact with members of the opposite sex.

These pleasurable effects of cocaine last only a few minutes. Within fifteen minutes users often lose the high and want more cocaine.[2] After repeated use of cocaine, the pleasurable feelings

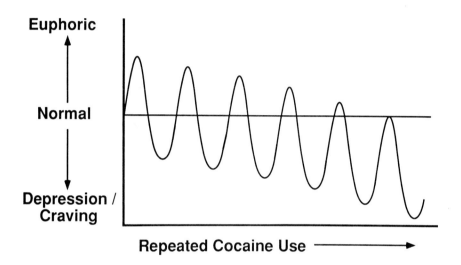

With repeated cocaine use, the highs become less intense and the depression and craving following cocaine use generally increase in intensity. Ultimately, regular cocaine use is needed for a person to feel "normal."

are less frequent and less intense, and the need for cocaine increases. The unpleasant feelings when cocaine's effects wear off become more intense after repeated use. Some users have said that when they first start using cocaine, a memory is created for an intensely pleasurable experience. Users keep taking more cocaine with the hope of capturing that pleasurable experience. That feeling, however, can never be recaptured. Repeated cocaine use results in less and less enjoyment.

Shortly after a run of cocaine use ends, the user may feel irritable, depressed, and tired. Heavy users may experience serious mood disturbances that resemble a form of mental illness called schizophrenia.[3] These individuals will feel that everyone is against them, a feeling called paranoia. Paranoid users will become suspicious and lose trust in people, even those they are close to. They may experience hallucinations, reporting that they see, hear, or feel things that are not there. A common report is that there are bugs crawling under the skin. Users will scratch and injure their skin when they feel these sensations.[4]

How Does Cocaine Affect Behavior?

Cocaine causes several noticeable changes in behavior. These same changes in behavior have been studied in the animal laboratory. The types of changes in behavior and the extent to which they change will depend on the environment or surroundings. Changes in behavior that are most often seen are increased motion, pacing, and nervousness.

The effects of cocaine also depend on the dose, how much was taken, and whether it was taken with any other drug. At a low dose, cocaine may speed up behavior and at a high dose it may slow it down. Very different effects may result depending upon whether a person is taking cocaine for the first time, occasionally, or on a regular basis. Finally, how cocaine is taken is important. Cocaine that is injected into a vein will have a very different effect than cocaine that is snorted.

One example of cocaine's effects is increased activity. After cocaine is taken, the user may seem more restless or fidgety. He or she may be unable to stand or sit for long periods of time. He or she may pace instead of patiently waiting for something, or seem in a hurry to complete a task. Cocaine may cause the user to overreact to people or events in the environment, such as a phone or doorbell ringing.

Sometimes cocaine use results in stereotyped or compulsive behavior. This refers to behavior that is repeated over and over again. It might take the form of picking or rubbing the skin. There may also be compulsive checking behavior, like repeatedly checking to see if a door is locked or looking for something. In laboratory animals, cocaine may produce grooming behavior, rocking or pacing in the cage, or biting on the cage floor or on objects protruding into the cage.

The third type of behavior that is characteristic of cocaine use is aggression. Users often appear irritable, hostile, and short-tempered. There may be a mistrust of family members and friends. Cocaine alone does not produce aggression. It seems to make people more sensitive to events in the environment that might trigger aggression. Aggression and poor judgement during cocaine use may be related to serious social problems. In New York City, for instance, up to one-fourth of all drivers killed in car accidents tested positive for cocaine. Up to one-third of the murders in New York City occurred in those involved in the cocaine trade, although all of those who trade cocaine are not

27

necessarily users.[5] Most murders were due to territory wars among drug dealers.[6]

It is a common belief that cocaine use causes people to be more aggressive and commit crimes, but there is no way to prove this. Not many laboratory studies of cocaine use and aggression have been conducted on people. In one laboratory study human volunteers were asked to give electric shocks to another "volunteer." There was not really a person there receiving shocks. When volunteers were given cocaine, they delivered higher shock levels.[7] Several aggression studies have been conducted on animals and the results are not that clear. In animal studies researchers have studied attack and biting behavior that occurs when animals are given an electric shock. In squirrel monkeys, low and medium doses of cocaine increase the amount of aggression after an electric shock. Very high doses decrease aggression or attack behavior. In mice and pigeons, cocaine decreases aggression produced by shock. So, cocaine does not have a simple effect on aggression. It depends on the environmental conditions, the dose, and the type of animal being tested.

Long-term use of cocaine can lead to problems in getting along with other people. When users begin to spend most of their time purchasing and using cocaine, work, school, family life, and friendships suffer. Often users steal or become dealers to pay for their habit and get into trouble with the legal system. As users take more cocaine, they may become depressed, anxious, and irritable. These are behaviors that further distance them from family and friends. Then they may feel there is no one to turn to for help. When cocaine use is stopped, users often report that they cannot find pleasure in activities that had been enjoyable before. These negative feelings may lead a person to take more cocaine for temporary relief.

How Addictive is Cocaine?

Cocaine is a highly addictive drug. It has several features that make it so addictive. First, it can give a person a high or a feeling of well-being. Second, its effects begin very quickly after the drug is taken. It can be snorted through the nose, smoked, or injected into the veins (intravenously). Its peak effects can occur within five seconds.[8] This rapid action produces what is called a rush or a sudden change of feelings. This fast action greatly adds to the pleasurable feelings. These feelings are called the rewarding effects of a drug. If cocaine is taken by mouth, it will eventually have similar effects on the mind and body, but the beginning of these effects will be less intense and felt more gradually.[9] For this reason, cocaine is not usually taken by mouth.

The difference in how long it takes a drug to work, depending on how it is taken, might be compared to this example: A twelve-story drop on a roller coaster might take three seconds, but a twelve-story drop on a sloping mountain road might take five minutes. Both give a person the feeling of losing altitude and a change in sensation. The roller coaster, like smoked or snorted cocaine, would also produce more of a rush or thrill.

A third feature of cocaine is that its effects last a short time. Fifteen minutes after smoking or intravenous (IV) use, the effects quickly begin to wear off. Shorter acting drugs seem to be more addicting than long acting ones. For example, amphetamine (also known as speed) has many effects that are similar to

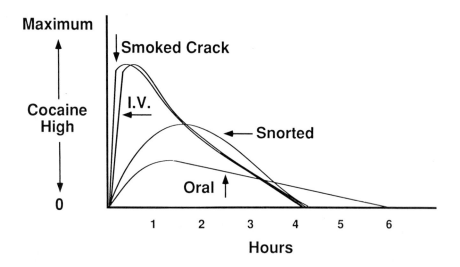

The speed at which cocaine's effects are felt, the intensity of those effects, and how long they will last depends on how the drug is used.

cocaine. Its slow beginning and long-lasting action however, make it less addicting than cocaine.

There is another indicator of a drug's ability to cause addiction. Does the user become hooked after the first time he or she uses it? There certainly have been reports on TV and in magazines suggesting a user may become addicted to cocaine after only one use. However, this question is difficult to test on human volunteers. Researchers cannot study illegal drugs of abuse on people who are not already users.[10]

One way to answer the question of how addicting a particular drug can be is with animal research. In a relatively minor operation, animals can have a tube implanted in one of their veins. This procedure is similar to having an intravenous or IV tube placed in your arm in the hospital. The animals with the IV tube are then trained to press a bar. By doing this they receive an automatic injection of cocaine through their tube. This is one way of finding out how much an animal likes a drug. How hard is the animal willing to work for the drug? The work is measured by how many times the animal will press a bar for that drug. If an animal presses a bar many times for cocaine, laboratory evidence suggests that cocaine is highly addicting.[11] The results of these studies show that the more cocaine an animal receives as a result of bar pressing, the harder he works. Eventually, when the dose gets very high, the animal is too intoxicated to keep up the high rate of bar pressing. He may then show stereotyped behavior, like repeatedly rocking or biting the cage floor, and lever pressing declines.

Another measure of the addiction potential of a drug is the number of animals that will push a bar for drug injections. If only half of a group of animals are interested in pressing a bar for

31

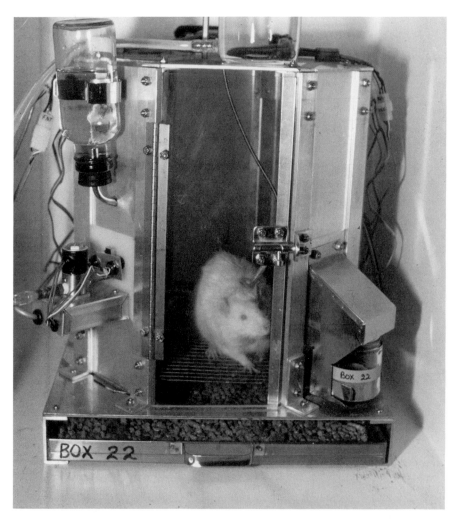

The rat in this picture is taking part in a test to determine how often it will perform a given task in order to receive a reward of cocaine. Since we can not legally administer cocaine and crack to humans who are not already users, this test allows us to study factors that cause the initiation of cocaine use.

a drug, that drug is probably less addicting than if 100 percent of the animals will press the bar.[12] Close to 100 percent of the rats or monkeys tested will press a bar for cocaine. This is another indicator of its high addiction potential. In fact, cocaine is one of the easiest drugs to get an animal to take on its own.

Recently, researchers have been testing animals to find out how addicting different drugs are. The animals must choose between a drug such as cocaine and a nondrug reward like a sweet drink or food. If the drug is not very addicting, the animals might choose the drug and nondrug reward almost equally. With cocaine, the choice is almost always greater for the drug. Under certain conditions, when the animal has very limited access to cocaine and food, it will choose only cocaine, and its health will begin to deteriorate.[13]

This behavior is also seen in human users. When a cocaine-addicted individual has a limited income or no income, often all of their resources are used for buying cocaine. Cocaine addiction is more common among inner-city groups with low income than in those groups with high income. However, there are some examples of people with big incomes who give up cars, houses, healthy diets, and contact with wives, husbands, children, and friends to pursue their cocaine habit. In these cases, cocaine is often chosen over all other nondrug rewards in their environment. What we have learned from animal and human behavior is that having other nondrug rewarding activities is a good way to stay away from drugs.

How Difficult Is It to Stop Using Cocaine?

For regular cocaine and crack users it is very difficult to stop using cocaine. For these users it is usually lack of money, imprisonment for cocaine-related crimes, and/or severe physical or mental illness that stops crack use. Of the heavy users who go through treatment, more than eighty out of one hundred are back to heavy cocaine use within six months.[14] Addiction to other stimulant drugs such as nicotine is equally hard to treat. Often several rounds of treatment and different styles of treatment are necessary to successfully stop these addictions. Positive results are possible if the user is well educated about his or her addiction and highly motivated to stop. At the present time, policy makers feel that it is so difficult to stop heavy cocaine use that more effort and money should be put into preventing it.

On the other hand, there are some users, perhaps as many as 60 percent who use cocaine less frequently. Instead of being high on cocaine most of the time, these users may smoke crack only a few times a day. There are others who use it only during weekends or a few times a month. It is not known why some are occasional users and others are heavy users. However, the trend is to go from lighter use to heavy use. One almost never goes from heavy use to occasional use. The more regular cocaine use becomes, the more difficult it is to stop. The same pattern is seen with cigarettes in teens. It is easiest to stop smoking within the first year before use becomes heavy and regular behavioral patterns are formed. After someone has smoked for a year or more, it is very difficult to stop.

What Are the Long-term Effects of Cocaine?

Very little is known about how much cocaine use is necessary to produce damaging effects on the body and brain. However, there are indicators that changes in brain chemistry take place right after cocaine use and may last for at least several weeks or more after cocaine use has stopped.

Another change is called neuroadaptation or tolerance and dependence. It means that the brain adjusts the amount of chemicals it produces depending on how the drug changes those chemicals. If cocaine makes more of a chemical in the brain, called dopamine, available to the brain cells, the brain cells that produce dopamine may decrease in number. When cocaine use is abruptly stopped, there will be disturbed behavioral and physical effects because the brain is not able to make its normal amount of dopamine yet. There are changes called tolerance and dependence that suggest that brain chemicals have been changed.[15]

Tolerance

Tolerance to a drug occurs when the effects decrease after it is administered repeatedly. This results in the user taking higher and higher doses to get the same effect that was first experienced. The opposite of tolerance is sensitization. When this happens cocaine's effects become stronger each time the individual uses the drug. Both tolerance and sensitization have been reported with the use of cocaine. There may be tolerance or sensitization to differing effects of the drug. For instance, there may be tolerance to the ability of cocaine to produce pleasurable effects, increased body temperature, increased heart rate, and loss of appetite. These effects decrease slightly each time cocaine is taken. On the other hand, users may become sensitized to some of the toxic effects such as the suspicion and fear (paranoia) that accompanies cocaine use. There is a rapid type of tolerance that develops with cocaine use that is called acute tolerance or tachyphylaxis. When several snorts or smokes of cocaine are

taken over a short time period, at first there is a rapid increase in heart rate, blood pressure, and feelings of "high." When the third or fourth doses are taken an hour or so later, these effects are greatly reduced. Cocaine users learn to space their use of the drug to avoid this rapid tolerance effect. Not a lot is known about tolerance effects in human users, because they have not been carefully studied in the laboratory. Reports from experiences on the street are often unreliable because the user is not sure of the actual dose he or she is getting due to impurities and the addition of other substances to cocaine.

More is known about tolerance and sensitivity to cocaine through animal studies. Whether tolerance or sensitivity develops may depend on several factors: (1) the dose of cocaine that is regularly taken, (2) the type of behavior or physical change that is being measured, and (3) the frequency at which the drug is given. Animal research has shown a mixture of results: tolerance, no effect, or sensitization with repeated cocaine exposure. A general trend is that when low cocaine doses are taken, more and more is needed to get an effect (tolerance). When high doses are taken, an individual can become sensitive and react more strongly each time the same high dose is taken. Cross tolerance occurs when exposure to one drug produces tolerance to a second drug. There is cross tolerance between cocaine and similar stimulant drugs such as amphetamine, methamphetamine (ice), and methylphenidate (Ritalin™), a drug used for hyperactivity and attention deficit disorder.

Dependence

Dependence occurs as the body adapts to the presence of a drug. Changes in the neurochemical activity of the brain occur to adapt to the chemical changes brought on by the drug. The brain may become more sensitive or less sensitive to certain chemicals as the drug is repeatedly used. When regular use of the drug is stopped, the brain has to readapt to the neurochemical imbalance. One way to determine whether a person is dependent upon a drug is to observe the effect when the drug is taken away. Usually the result is the opposite effect of the drug. For instance, a drug like alcohol or heroin slows down behavior so when it is taken away, the result might be restlessness or agitation. This is called a drug withdrawal symptom.

Since cocaine speeds up behavior, withdrawal symptoms are tiredness and desire to sleep. Withdrawal symptoms usually last for a few days. They will immediately disappear if the person uses cocaine again. When the cocaine is removed and there are withdrawal symptoms that can be reversed by giving the person the cocaine, it is certain that physical dependence has developed.

With some drugs like alcohol or heroin the withdrawal symptoms resemble an illness. There are chills, fever, stomach cramps, nausea, and vomiting. Cocaine withdrawal does not produce these visible symptoms. There are three phases of cocaine withdrawal.[16] During the first phase, which lasts several days, there is a feeling of depression, craving for cocaine, and an excessive amount of sleeping and eating. The second phase, which may last for several weeks, produces feelings of anxiety, depression, a lack of pleasure in normally preferred activities, and lack of motivation, or boredom. There is also difficulty in concentrating on thoughts and tasks. Suicide may occur during this phase. During the third phase a person's mood is steadier, except for occasional episodes of strong cocaine craving. For months, even years, after someone stops using cocaine, craving for cocaine can still occur. Craving can be triggered by the sight

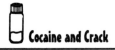

of people, places, or things that were previously related to cocaine use.

Recent studies with animals have shown that cocaine dependence can develop after very few exposures to cocaine. Animals are trained to work on a lever or other device for food. They are required to respond many times for each piece of food. At the same time the animals are exposed to daily injections of cocaine. When cocaine is removed, working for food is greatly decreased. If the animals are handed food they will eat, but they will not work hard for food. The animals do not appear to be ill during cocaine withdrawal, but their motivation for survival activities has been decreased. This may last for several weeks. Human cocaine users also report long-term decreases in motivation after cocaine use is stopped. This suggests that treatment for cocaine abuse would need to be carried out for a long period of time.

Irreversible Effects

Research has shown irreversible effects with other stimulant drugs that are similar to cocaine such as amphetamine (speed) and methamphetamine. The chemicals in the brain (dopamine) that increase when a stimulant drug like cocaine is taken are thought to produce the good feelings or a high. When researchers study the brains of rats that have had amphetamines for a long time, even long after they have stopped using amphetamines, they find a decrease in dopamine. They have also found that some brain cells in the pleasure center of the brain have died. Once brain cells have died, the brain cannot grow new ones. If this happens in humans, it may explain the long term craving for a drug and inability to experience pleasure.

Similar studies have been conducted with rats exposed to cocaine. The results have been mixed. Some show long-lasting changes in amounts of important neurochemicals such as dopamine and serotonin, but others report only short-term effects. The normal dopamine and serotonin levels return. More research is needed to resolve this discrepancy. Recent studies suggest that there may be depression and loss of memory and concentration that last several weeks or more after cocaine use has stopped.[17] We must rely on the animal data to answer this question. It is too expensive and impractical to follow cocaine users for many years to determine whether there are permanent changes in mood and behavior.

Is Cocaine Use Related to Mental Illness?

There is a theory that individuals with mental disorders like depression or anxiety are more likely to abuse cocaine because it relieves their symptoms. There are certainly data suggesting that there is more mental illness in cocaine users than the rest of the population. There is also more cocaine and drug abuse in the mentally ill than in the rest of the population. While this relationship is interesting, we do not know what causes it. Does mental illness cause drug abuse or does drug abuse cause mental illness? There may be a third factor such as a socially or economically impoverished environment or heredity that causes both.

Attempts have been made to treat cocaine abuse by treating an underlying mental illness such as depression. Although antidepressant drugs were slightly effective in some studies, in later studies they have had little effect on cocaine abuse. Most drug treatments have the goal of reducing the discomfort of cocaine withdrawal. At that time there is often depression, unpleasant feelings, and an inability to experience pleasure. Antidepressant drugs have been used successfully for depression. Drugs that reduce craving are somewhat helpful. Drugs that stimulate dopamine release have eased cocaine withdrawal. Most of these drugs have a moderate effect during the cocaine withdrawal phase. There is little evidence that they are successful at keeping users off cocaine for a long time.

Since the days of Sigmund Freud, there has been the idea that cocaine could be used to treat mental disorders. It does produce a brief improvement in depressed mood. It allows people like entertainers and athletes to perform when they have been without sleep for a long time. Cocaine has not been used medically for these purposes for a long time. The reason is the unpleasant effects (restlessness, depression, paranoia) and the risk of addiction that outweigh the beneficial effects of the drug.

Another connection between cocaine and mental illness is that at high doses or after long, heavy use cocaine can produce a mental disorder that is like paranoid schizophrenia. A paranoid schizophrenic may hallucinate and feel that others are plotting to harm him or her. Researchers thought cocaine could be used to create a model of this disorder in animals. They could then test drugs or other treatment methods to reduce the symptoms. This line of research has been disappointing because it has not led to the development of new treatment medications.

How Does Cocaine Affect the Body?

One indicator of the harmful effects of cocaine is the estimates from the Drug Abuse Warning Network (DAWN)[18] of the number of emergency room episodes related to a certain kind of drug use. In 1978 when this type of reporting began, there were 3,500 cocaine-related episodes. In 1984 when crack use began there were 24,500 episodes, and in 1992 there was an all-time high, 119,800 cocaine-related episodes. This was a 20 percent increase over the last five years. These estimates do not include information about the specific physical or mental complaints that brought people into the emergency room. They simply indicate that cocaine use was reported.

Cocaine affects many important bodily systems such as the brain (central nervous system), the heart (cardiovascular system), the digestive system, and the reproductive system. There are secondary effects such as malnutrition which result because cocaine use reduces appetite. Also energy and money that would have been spent obtaining food go to cocaine rather than food in the regular user. There are also special effects related to the way cocaine is used. If it is injected, there may be sores on the skin that result from repeated needle sticks. When cocaine is injected under the skin, small amounts of skin tissue die and become infected.

Snorting cocaine causes special problems for the mucous membranes in the nose. Individuals who regularly use cocaine this way may have swollen, irritated tissue in their nose resulting in a constant runny nose and congestion. In severe cases, enough tissue destruction may occur that this condition remains permanently even if cocaine use is stopped. There may also be loss of smell. The health problems that are related to smoking are a constant cough and upper bronchitis type of respiratory inflammation.

One of the worst consequences of injecting cocaine is AIDS, which can result from needle sharing. Although people are

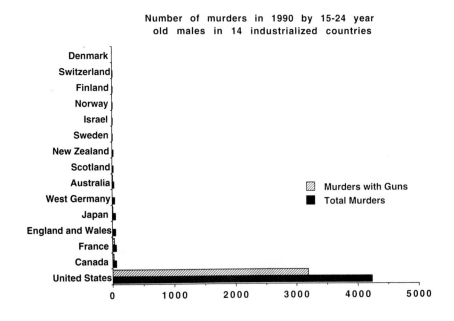

Number of murders in 1990 by 15-24 year
old males in 14 industrialized countries

Denmark
Switzerland
Finland
Norway
Israel
Sweden
New Zealand
Scotland
Australia
West Germany
Japan
England and Wales
France
Canada
United States

⬚ Murders with Guns
■ Total Murders

0   1000   2000   3000   4000   5000

One consequence of the poor judgement associated with cocaine abuse is an
increased murder rate. Gun-realted murders among males between the ages of
fifteen and twenty–four are thousands of times higher in the United States than in
any of the fourteen other industrialized nations of the world.

generally aware that needle sharing is responsible for the spread of AIDS, hepatitis, and other diseases, judgement is clouded when one is intoxicated or craving cocaine. Although in the United States AIDS was a disease that was initially spread among homosexual men, it has now spread to women through needle sharing and sex with infected partners. This has been devastating because many children with AIDS are born to women who contracted the disease through cocaine abuse and needle sharing. In some large cities like New York, the government has attempted to combat this problem by establishing needle exchange programs. Dirty needles can be exchanged for clean ones with no questions asked. Cocaine use has also resulted in the spread of AIDS and other sexually-transmitted diseases because of an increasing trend among women to trade sexual favors for crack. Unfortunately, younger and younger adolescents are getting involved in this practice as a means of supporting their cocaine habit.

Cocaine Effects On the Brain

The most serious effect of cocaine on the brain is that it might cause a paralyzing stroke or sudden death. This may result because a large increase in blood pressure causes bleeding in the brain. Another way cocaine causes brain damage is by a blockage of blood and oxygen to the brain. This happens because cocaine constricts blood vessels, and causes them to shrink. Because cocaine's effects on blood pressure last only about fifteen minutes, by the time a cocaine user is brought to the emergency room with a stroke, it is not possible to determine what the specific cause was.

Another of cocaine's effects on the brain is seizures. They

happen because cocaine produces very high body temperatures. High temperatures can result in seizures. Seizures may also result because of abnormalities in heart function such as very rapid beating (fibrillation). Laboratory studies with rats suggest that cocaine makes individuals more prone to seizures by making nerve cells in the brain more sensitive to events that can trigger seizures. Seizures may be fatal or cause brain damage if they persist for an hour or more.[19] They may be stopped with treatment drugs if the person is taken to the hospital for treatment in time. Strokes and seizures do not occur in all users, but they occur more frequently than in people who do not use cocaine.

It is rare that cocaine causes enough damage to the brain to result in stroke or seizures. A much more common form of damage is a change in brain chemicals that leads to behavioral problems and mood disorders. Dopamine is a chemical that is involved in sensations of pleasure. Cocaine causes the nerve cells in the brain to be exposed to more dopamine by allowing it to stay around the nerve cells longer. That is why cocaine makes people feel good. Since dopamine stays in between nerve cells longer, after a while there may be fewer cells making dopamine. This may explain the feelings of sadness and depression that occur when a person stops taking cocaine. There is no cocaine to increase dopamine levels and fewer cells are making it naturally. The only way out of the depression is to take more cocaine. So cocaine is taken to feel good and to not feel bad. After an extended period of cocaine use, cocaine can no longer produce the intense good feelings, and users take it just to feel normal. In a way, cocaine eventually reduces the ability of the brain to experience pleasure. Many users report that people or events that once were pleasurable are no longer, and cocaine is the only way to get a little pleasure. Scientists believe that cocaine changes the way the brain works, but they are not yet sure of exactly how it is changed and whether or not the changes are permanent.

Another serious effect of cocaine on the brain is in behavioral problems. They may be in the form of depression, nervousness, poor judgement, or antisocial behavior. These problems are difficult because they do not allow a person to function normally in society. They often lead to loss of job, spouse, and custody of children. In heavy cocaine users, behavioral problems may result from a mental disorder called psychosis. Signs of this disorder are excessive worry, paranoia, and difficulty distinguishing between what is real and what is not. In some users there may be hallucinations, or violent episodes. There may also be senseless, repetitive gestures called stereotyped behavior. An example might be pacing or picking one's skin.

There are also less severe behavior changes that occur in most cocaine users. These may also be telltale signs to parents and friends that someone is using cocaine and needs help. Moderate or even occasional cocaine users may seem hyperactive and irritable. They may develop repetitive patterns of behavior, or rituals. They may frequently indicate that someone is watching them or speaking unkindly about them. They may lose interest in eating or sleep poorly when on cocaine. In contrast, they may sleep for long periods of time when they have just gone off cocaine, and they may be very hungry when they awaken. These behaviors are all present in normal cocaine-free individuals at one time or another. It is their increased frequency that makes them seem abnormal.

Cocaine's Effect On the Heart and Lungs

Cocaine makes your heart beat faster. It reduces the size of your blood vessels, and this makes your blood flow faster. This also causes your blood pressure to rise, and in extreme cases these changes in heart function can cause a heart attack. Cocaine's ability to produce sudden death is due to its effect on the heart and blood supply. Heart attacks have occurred in young cocaine users shortly after a cocaine binge. In most of these patients, the arteries leading to the heart are blocked, but about a third of the patients have normal arteries. The average age of crack users who have heart attacks is thirty-one. This is much younger than the usual age of heart attack patients which is usually after the age of fifty. This suggests that cocaine acts directly on the heart, not the blood vessels. A number of reports suggest that cocaine disrupts the rhythm of the heart (ventricular arrhythmia), and this effect has been demonstrated in the laboratory with dogs.[20] Sudden death may also be caused by slowed breathing and convulsions caused by lack of oxygen to the lungs, heart, and brain. Cocaine can also interfere with the signals in your brain that tell your lungs to breathe. This may stop or slow your breathing and cause death. Cocaine also causes your body temperature to rise. Some experts believe this may be one of the causes of death after cocaine use.

The effects of cocaine on the heart are difficult to study for many reasons. First, the effect has usually worn off by the time the person is brought to the emergency room. Cocaine can be measured in the urine and in hair samples, but the amounts do not reflect how much cocaine a person took. Also, low doses have different effects than high doses. Other drugs or impurities may have been combined with the cocaine. Street drugs almost always have impurities or other cheaper drugs added. Finally, your heart function is regulated by many factors, including electrical impulses, muscle tone, rhythm or pacemaker activity, and chemicals in the blood. More research is needed to find which one of these heart functions is most affected by cocaine use. Many cocaine users also smoke cigarettes, so it is difficult to determine what the effects of cocaine alone would be. Cocaine can make asthma worse. One study reported that a third of crack smokers wheeze while smoking. There have also been reports of "crack lung" which is like a cough with chest pain.

Cocaine's Effects On the Digestive System

Cocaine may cause damage to your intestines, liver, and kidneys. Some people lack an enzyme (pseudocholinesterase) that is necessary for the digestion and elimination of cocaine. In these people, cocaine can build up to dangerous levels very fast. In people who lack this enzyme, cocaine may cause more toxic effects to the digestive system than to the brain and heart. When cocaine and alcohol are used together there is also increased liver damage.

Effects On Children of Cocaine Users

Most drugs that women take while pregnant enter the fetus's blood through the umbilical cord. Cocaine is no exception, in fact it passes rather rapidly from mother to baby. Since the baby is much smaller than the mother, the dose that the mother takes to get high is a very large dose for the baby. There is an enzyme called cholinesterase that helps eliminate cocaine from the body.

Women have less of this than men, so cocaine has a stronger effect on women. Fetuses have very little cholinesterase. So, it is very hard for them to get rid of the cocaine that enters their body through the umbilical cord.

The use of cocaine by women of childbearing age has increased in recent years. This trend has introduced a concern for the effect of cocaine on babies and developing children. In some states pregnant cocaine users are held in jail until their babies are born, to protect the unborn child from cocaine exposure. Children of cocaine-using mothers have been called "crack babies" by TV and magazine reporters. It is an unfortunate label because we do not know yet whether these children will suffer any long-term effects because their mothers used crack. Initial studies suggested that cocaine-exposed babies were also addicted, that they were irritable, and that they did not bond well with others. More recent studies suggest that as these babies grow, they catch up and soon are no different than other children in their particular environment.

There are other factors that could explain these effects in babies of cocaine-using mothers. Poor nutrition or exposure to pollutants in the work or home environment may be responsible. If the mothers smoke cigarettes or drink alcohol in addition to using cocaine, this also results in lower birth weight, premature birth and small head size. There may also be neglect of the child's nutritional and medical needs in the home of a cocaine-abusing parent.

Recent studies have shown that the cocaine-exposed babies who are born with low birth weight and/or head size catch up to normal children between three months and twenty-four months. The long term effects of cocaine exposure before birth are not known. Studies with rats and monkeys show similar complications with the birth process and low birth weight that catches up. However, researchers have not yet found major effects on development, learning and performance in animals.[21] One animal study suggests that the effect of cocaine exposure may surface in old age or when the animal is stressed in some way such as by exposure to a toxic substance. The effects of cocaine may only be seen when they are combined with other stressful events.

Interactions With Other Drugs

Very few cocaine users take only cocaine. Cocaine is often taken with legal drugs such as caffeine, nicotine or alcohol. It may also be taken with prescription drugs that affect behavior. Many users deliberately take cocaine along with other illegal drugs such as heroin to get a different type of experience. The two drugs most commonly used with cocaine are heroin and alcohol.

Speedballs

Cocaine users often take heroin to balance the high degree of stimulation caused by cocaine. This combination is called a speedball. The combination allows the cocaine user to experience the effects of cocaine and also to be able to relax or sleep. For some users the combination is more pleasurable than either drug alone. Unfortunately the combination of these drugs may be more toxic and deadly than either used alone. For instance, heroin slows down breathing sometimes too low for the brain to get enough oxygen. Cocaine may have that effect too at high doses. When they are combined sudden death may result even though the user is taking amounts of cocaine and heroin that he or she

has used safely, separately, in the past. John Belushi, a well-known comedian during the 1970s and early 1980s, died from speedballing.

Cocaethylene

Recent studies have reported that six to nine out of every ten cocaine abusers are also alcohol abusers.[22] Nine out of ten of the cocaine-alcohol abusers use the two drugs simultaneously. When a person takes cocaine and alcohol (ethanol) together, a new substance is formed called cocaethylene or ethylcocaine.[23] Cocaethylene is as strong as cocaine and acts very much like cocaine in the body. So, when a user takes cocaine and alcohol it may be like taking a double dose of cocaine. It could become a deadly combination. Cocaethylene lasts longer than cocaine and may have more serious effects on the heart. Cocaine users intentionally use this combination because it prolongs the cocaine "high". Alcohol also seems to reduce some of the negative effects of cocaine such as agitation and paranoia. In some cocaine users, alcohol reduces the negative effects of withdrawal especially during the crash phase. The Drug Abuse Warning Network (DAWN) reported in 1991 and 1992 that the number of emergency room cases showing cocaethylene in the blood is higher than cocaine alone. It is the most common combination of two drugs that results in death. Laboratory experiments with animals[24] and human subjects[25] have shown that cocaethylene is more toxic than cocaine alone.

Cocaine Overdose and Its Treatment

There are several types of toxicity that can occur if a person takes too much cocaine. Cocaine overdose mainly affects the central nervous system or brain. But, it could also result in heart damage, stroke, seizures, or sudden death. After taking too much cocaine, a person may first feel stimulated and euphoric. This quickly gives way to excitement, restlessness, and nervousness. Next, there may be nausea, vomiting, and stomachache. Muscle twitching may be noticed. Blood pressure increases, heart rate increases, and the skin color may look pale. In the next phase there may be seizures and heartbeat irregularities. Breathing becomes faster and deeper. Late, breathing gradually slows, the circulatory system collapses, and death follows.

There is currently no drug that will block or reverse a cocaine overdose. Each symptom is treated as it happens. The goal is to keep the patient alive until the drug wears off. Sedatives are administered to relax the overdose patient. Drugs to slow and stabilize heart rate and lower blood pressure are given with caution because they may interact with cocaine. Antiseizure drugs may be given to prevent or stop seizures. New drugs are currently being developed that will break down cocaine more quickly than the body can naturally. These have been successful in animal studies. Fortunately, cocaine's effects are short-lived. The toxic effects of an overdose may disappear within six hours. Death due to cocaine overdose occurs only in a small percentage of users. Most cocaine-related deaths are from the trauma of the environment a cocaine user lives in. A review of the United States Coroners' reports revealed that more cocaine-related deaths are due to murder, suicide, and accidents than to the medical complications of cocaine itself.[26] Many of the murders are due to dealers fighting over territories.

Questions for Discussion

1. Do you think one-time cocaine use can result in addiction?

2. Why do you think cocaine use makes a person violent?

3. How can you tell if a friend is using cocaine?

4

Social Aspects of Cocaine Abuse

Role of Society in General

In the past, society in general has had a great influence on the spread of cocaine and other drug abuse. Information about drugs came mainly from doctors or from suggestions of home remedies from friends and family. When drugs like cocaine, morphine, and heroin were first introduced, the doctors said they were safe and had many benefits and few risks. It is difficult to change these attitudes even as the negative effects become more well-known. There is also a tendency to forget history. Cocaine use was nearly stopped after the Harrison Narcotic Act of 1914, but by the 1970s, when amphetamine abuse was widespread, cocaine was announced as a safer alternative than amphetamine (speed). The following is one example of many positive stories about cocaine that appeared in the newspapers and magazines:

"Most of the evidence is that there aren't any adverse effects to normal cocaine use. It looks to be much safer than barbiturates and amphetamines . . ." (*San Francisco Chronicle*, October 21, 1976, page 4).

A new epidemic starting with snorting and then leading to crack smoking began in the 1980s.

At the present time, society in general has so many ways of influencing a person's decision to use or not use drugs that it is impossible to identify the most important influence. The table below shows a list of factors that may influence a person in either direction. Some of them actually cancel each other out, such as friends that encourage drug use and other friends who discourage use. It is probably the sum of many of these forces in addition to individual personality that determines the end result.

Factors Controlling Drug Abuse

Promotes drug abuse	Protects against drug abuse
Lack of law enforcement	Laws, punishment
Low cost	High cost
Incentives	Drawbacks, side-effects
Drug-using role models	Drug-free role models
Lack of other activities	Church, school
Gangs	Social organizations
Peer pressure	Support of friends / family
TV shows, movies	TV public service
Alcohol and cigarette ads	Billboards, magazine ads

Does the Environment Create Cocaine Abuse?

There are many factors that may cause an individual to use cocaine. The environment, the family, personality, and economic status all play a role in determining whether a person will use drugs. There is no magic formula that can be used to determine whether or not a person will become a cocaine addict. The more factors that exist for a person, the more likely it is that he or she will become addicted. Of course, there are exceptions. Some individuals may have all of the conditions that usually result in cocaine abuse and not become addicted. Researchers would be very interested to find out what prevents that type of individual from becoming a user.[1]

Young teens who live in an environment with factors such as: easy access to cocaine, many young cocaine users, very few other rewarding or enjoyable opportunities, and few parents or elders around to supervise are likely to use cocaine or other drugs.[2] Urban slums are a place where these conditions typically exist, but they are also present in upper-middle-class housing areas as well. These are conditions where both parents are working and teens may be ignored or isolated. They are not encouraged to participate in other activities, and cocaine may be cheap and easy to obtain.

More teens with lower economic status than those with higher economic status use cocaine. Crack cocaine is inexpensive, and that is a major factor promoting its use. In New York City, ten dollars can buy enough crack for about three uses. As a teen becomes a regular user, he or she rapidly becomes involved in dealing (selling to others). Teens quickly learn that they can

55

make enough money dealing drugs to cover the cost of their own habit. Some dealers or distributors can make large amounts of money before they get caught by the police. This allows inner-city youth to have clothes, jewelry, and cars that they would never have been able to purchase with a regular job.

There is a great incentive to become involved with cocaine trade. But, the risk is high because there are severe penalties and prison terms for dealers who are caught.[3] Under federal drug laws, possession of cocaine can lead to a one-year prison term, but dealing can result in forty years or more depending upon whether the dealer is a repeat offender. Unfortunately, the dealers on the street who have not been caught are highly visible to the youth in the community. The dealers who have been caught are in prison and are not seen.

Studies seem to agree that a poor environment encourages drug abuse. A poor environment can be defined in many ways. For the inner-city slum resident there is a lack of material goods. There is often a single parent home, lack of self-worth, and little hope for the future. In many neighborhoods the only way to make money is to deal drugs. The poverty in an upper or middle class neighborhood is not lack of money but may be a lack of love, low feelings of self-worth, and a sense of not belonging. However, even if all of the material goods are provided by parents who are too busy to interact with the teen, that teen may not feel needed or that they make a difference. Even celebrity drug users may have a poor environment in the sense that long hours of work with demanding travel schedules are restrictions to personal freedom. Although huge sums of money are made, entertainers and sports figures are limited by the lack of time they have to spend and enjoy their money. Their personal freedom is also restricted by the difficulty in going places and doing things that the rest of society enjoys doing without being recognized. Another type of poor environment is a war zone or a prison. These places offer very limited opportunities for enjoyment and have a high rate of drug abuse. For example, many soldiers used heroin during the Vietnam War, but they almost all stopped when they returned home to the United States.[4] The military currently has very strict anti-drug laws, and drug abuse was not a problem in the recent Middle East conflict.

What is the Role of Gateway Drugs?

A gateway drug is the drug young people are exposed to first. Usually alcohol, cigarettes, and marijuana are gateway drugs. Caffeine may also be a gateway drug depending upon how heavily and intentionally it is used. It would appear that society supports the use of gateway drugs. Although marijuana is illegal in most states, there is little prosecution for its use. Society seems to feel that it is a relatively harmless drug. Cigarettes are legal, although their use has fallen over the past twenty years. There are still smoking sections in some restaurants and other buildings. Smoking is allowed on international flights of many airlines. By approving gateway drugs, society gives a general approval of drug use.

It is thought that gateway drugs open the doors to a cycle of addiction. It is easy to use alcohol or cigarettes if they are around the house. When they are used regularly to relax or to improve social interactions, it becomes easier to try another drug that is less available or more costly. The pattern of drug use has been set and the cycle has been started. Many users cycle through four or

five drugs. Others may settle on one or two. Very few teenagers begin to use marijuana without first using alcohol or cigarettes. A recent study of more than seven thousand students in grades seven through twelve has shown that use of alcohol or cigarettes and then marijuana is a strong indicator of crack use especially in males.[5] The age at which a person begins to use a gateway drug is important. The younger the age when the gateway drug is used, the greater the chance that the user will later move on to marijuana and then cocaine or crack.

What Messages Does Society Send to Teens About Cocaine?

Society, mainly through the media, sends teens mixed messages about drugs. Cigarette ads and liquor ads on billboards and in magazines feature young people (probably in their late teens) having a good time with drugs. A recent study of preschool children revealed that Joe Camel™ from the cigarette ads was more well recognized than Mickey Mouse. A high percentage of three-year-olds know who Joe Camel™ is, and more children than adults can identify this character.[6]

In contrast, the media has generally taken a negative stand on cocaine use. There were a series of "Just say no" messages on TV during the late 1980s. TV commercials later used stronger messages, such as an egg frying and the message "This is your brain on drugs." There is, in fact, little scientific evidence of brain damage in the cocaine user. Recent public service announcements on TV have used rock groups and sports figures or actors to discuss the negative effects of cocaine from personal experience.

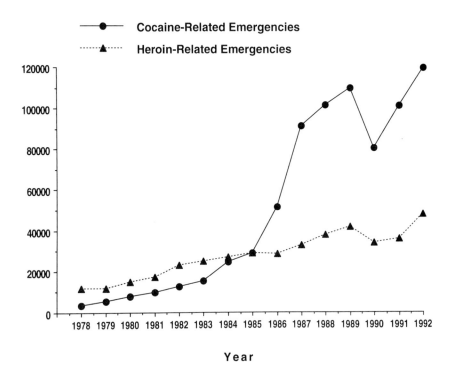

Cocaine- and crack-related emergencies increased dramatically from 1985 to 1992.

What Are the Best Ways to Prevent Cocaine Abuse?

Prevention efforts must begin very early with school children, because by sixth grade many children have begun to experiment with drugs. Smoking and alcohol use are common in middle and high schools. Prevention efforts there are aimed at telling students about the addictive nature of these substances. High school is a time when those who have begun somewhat regular drug use may stop more easily than a few years later when drug use is heavier and dependence on the drug is strong. Since alcohol and cigarette use often lead to use of illegal drugs, another goal of prevention efforts at the high school or early college level is to discourage the spread of drug use from gateway drugs to other substances. Those who go from alcohol and cigarettes to marijuana, for instance, are much more likely to use cocaine than those who do not use marijuana. The following sections will describe some ways of using education to prevent drug abuse.

Education Efforts

Education about the negative effects of drugs may not always lead to prevention. If you already know about drugs through parents or friends you may be convinced not to start. However, if you have not heard much about drugs you may find them interesting. Information about drug effects may make you curious and encourage you to experiment. An older study showed that the effect of drug education increased drug use two years after the educational program. However, students in the program were less likely to get into dangerous, heavy drug use than a group that did not receive the educational program. Drug education programs that are currently in use are designed to have one or more of the following goals or components:

To increase knowledge about short and long term effects of using drugs. Students learn about the effects of drugs on the body and behavior. The addictive aspects of drugs, such as tolerance, dependence, and relapse are described to students. Probably the most important fact about drugs is that shortly after regular use begins, the drug gains control over a person's behavior. Although intentions were to take it for a short time or only once in a while, changes in brain chemistry (tolerance, dependence) create a demand or craving for repeated use of the drug. Drug addiction is a disease, like diabetes or an allergy that needs to be treated to be kept under control.

To improve self-esteem or self-image. Specialists in the area of drug addiction believe that it is also important to talk about why you might take the drug. One of the main reasons is to change feelings about yourself. You may think that drugs make you feel accepted, powerful, or smart. You may think that drugs increase enjoyment of other pleasures in life. You may think that drugs tone down feelings of loneliness, disappointment, anxiety, or uselessness. Or you may take drugs to feel more stimulated and excited or to feel calm, relaxed, and less nervous. You can learn to change any of these feelings without the use of drugs.

To teach students to cope with teasing or peer pressure. Junior high students can be very hard on each other. This is a time when everyone is going through adolescence and feeling confused and insecure about many things. There is a tendency to release frustration by picking on others, teasing, ridiculing, and using put-downs. You can learn how to react so as not to encourage repeated attacks from others. You can also learn

61

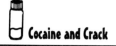

to be a more positive friend by avoiding put-downs and working together on projects that have good outcomes.

To role play situations that require saying no to drugs. The Reagan administration of the 1980s developed the concept of "Just say no" to drugs. Unfortunately, it is not that easy. Many educational programs include training in role-playing. Some students play the role of drug pushers and must use their best arguments to get non-users to use drugs. The non-users must practice ways of saying no while still saving face and maintaining friendships. These roles are switched so that everyone can practice saying no. Often theatre groups come to schools to help with role-playing. They can set up real-life situations and help you act in a convincing way when you practice saying no.

To substitute alternative activities for drug use. The alternative activities might be geared to the reason why drugs are taken. If they are taken because people have low self-esteem, doing things for other people may be an alternative. It makes people feel good to do things for others. If the goal of drug taking is relaxation, then exercise, reading, attending cultural events, movies, or socializing may be good substitutes. If drugs satisfy a desire for thrill-seeking or risk-taking, then sports or performing arts may prevent drug use. Finally, if drugs are taken to intensify thoughts or feelings in general, participating in religious or social activities may stimulate more interest in these matters.

Drug-free Schools

Another component in the educational process is a drug-free school.[7] Schools must apply for this status through an office in Washington, D.C. They must take the approach that drug use is

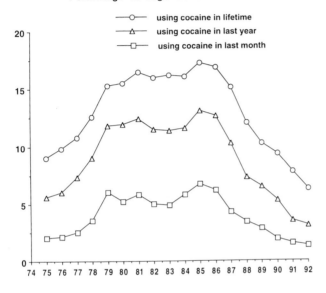

Percentage of High School Seniors

— ○ — using cocaine in lifetime
— △ — using cocaine in last year
— □ — using cocaine in last month

Year

From 1986 to 1992, there was a dramatic decrease in cocaine use among high school seniors in the United States.

wrong and harmful. Drugs, including tobacco and alcohol, are not allowed on school grounds or at activities that occur away from school. Teachers must not use tobacco, and they must use the drug-free message in their teaching. There must be educational programs for students and parents to encourage the drug-free lifestyle. Schools adopt severe penalties when drug use is discovered. Federal funding for other school programs may require that the school is drug-free. Schools must work very hard to obtain and keep this status. A team of evaluators comes from Washington to interview students, teachers, administrators, and parents before the drug-free school status is granted. They are closely monitored after that. Many schools are becoming drug-free in the 1990s. The attitude in the 1980s was that schools should not dictate social values. The increasing number of drug-free schools in the 1990s may be related to the reduced drug use reported in the Monitoring the Future Senior Survey that is sponsored by the Public Health Service.

The DARE Program

The Drug Abuse Resistance Education (DARE) program was started in 1983 in Los Angeles. It is now spreading rapidly all over the country. It is a program that starts in fifth and sixth grade and is run by police officers. They are in the classroom for an hour a day for seventeen weeks. They use many of the education methods already mentioned. They educate students about the biological effects of drugs. They train students in the areas of self-esteem and role-playing. They give sugestions about alternatives to drug use. Peer leaders are used and the teachers are also involved in some of the activities. The police are well informed in these areas. They also tell stories about their experience with drunken or drug-intoxicated drivers. There are workbooks and sometimes homework assignments. The students become very close to the DARE officers. There is a graduation ceremony attended by the officers, students, teachers, and parents. This is often a very emotional experience for all as the students make a commitment to stay away from drugs. Tee shirts, bumper stickers, and other prizes are awarded. There is usually a refresher course in the sixth grade. Often the DARE officers attend school functions or field trips to show the students they are interested in their progress. DARE is expensive, but it is a very popular and fast-growing program. Since it is relatively new, there is little information available about whether it will successfully prevent drug abuse.[8]

To date, most of the prevention programs including DARE that have been evaluated have yielded only small effects.[9] It may be necessary for them to start earlier and last longer. There are many opposing messages in families and environments. In the early years, drug use in the home environment may be a strong influence. Messages on TV and in the movies supporting drug use are very strong and may be hard to counteract.

Are There Different Rules For Different Ages and Different Drugs?

Part of the problem with educating young people about drugs is the mixed messages. Young people are told not to use drugs at all because legal drugs (tobacco and alcohol) are damaging to the body. They also may lead to addiction to other drugs like marijuana, heroin, or cocaine which will damage social relationships and the ability to work and be productive. High school and college students might be given the message to drink responsibly, use a designated (non-drinking) driver, or call a cab. Prevention efforts for students accept some drug use but warn users not to spread their use out to other more "dangerous" substances. Adults, on the other hand, are told where they can and cannot smoke. Alcohol ads talk about responsible *use*. These messages must be confusing to young teens. They are told to be drug-free, but they see older brothers, sisters, and parents using drugs. The message they are really getting is wait till you are older to use drugs. But is this the correct message? If drugs produce an addictive behavior pattern and craving that can last a lifetime, the goal for everyone should be to be drug-free.

Another confusing issue centers around the different types of drugs. As mentioned, tobacco and alcohol are damaging drugs to the body. However, they are legal for adults. Another problem is that caffeine, another drug, is freely available to children in soft drinks. In fact, it is hard to buy non-caffeinated drinks. Major fast-food chains and grocery stores usually offer many choices of caffeinated sodas, but only one or two less-desirable caffeine-free choices. Children learn very early that they are taking a drug in soda. It gives them pep and keeps them awake at night when their parents would like them to be sleeping. When they don't use caffeine for a while they notice that they are tired and may have a headache. This is a mild form of drug withdrawal. It must be confusing for a young person to be in a drug-free school that sells a drug in a soda machine.

The message keeps coming through that some drug use is acceptable. Actually, caffeine affects the brain and body in ways that are very similar to cocaine, only milder. Studies with rats show that experience with caffeine increases later acceptance of cocaine.[10] There is much we do not know about the interactions between drugs. There is some evidence that legal drugs serve as gateway drugs for illegal drugs. We do not know whether that is because changes have occurred in brain chemistry or cultural and behavioral patterns have been established. There may be a combination of factors.

What Are the Best Ways to Stop Cocaine Abuse?

There is not one single treatment method that works best for stopping cocaine abuse. Even under the best conditions most of those who stop taking cocaine will resume use soon after treatment ends. A combination of methods works better than one alone. There are methods designed to change behavior, to educate, and to offer alternative rewarding activities. There are also drugs that reduce the craving that occurs once cocaine use has stopped.

What is probably more important than the type of treatment is the timing of treatment. Treatment is most useful if it happens before cocaine use becomes heavy. Research in animal laboratories shows that both behavioral and drug treatments reduce drug taking early when the animals are taking only small amounts. Unfortunately, it is nearly impossible to convince a cocaine user to enter a treatment facility when he or she is an occasional user. The lack of regular use is the user's primary argument that there is not a problem.

Education Efforts

A great deal of money is spent educating the public on the dangers of cocaine use. Unfortunately, it is very difficult to measure the results. The High School Senior Survey shows cocaine use decreased slightly over the last several years. This may be due to better education efforts.

Community Efforts

Communities are recognizing that providing activities as alternatives to drug use is a successful strategy. Many recent studies agree that prevention may be successful with teens who are involved in other activities that are not compatible with drug use. Communities offer sports, arts, academic, or social activities after school, and these may satisfy the needs that could result in drug taking. However, they are not a guarantee of prevention.

Special Programs for High Risk Children

The limited success of many treatment programs has focused more attention on prevention. Identification of risk factors will help school counselors give extra help to those that are high risk. But in the public schools most of the prevention or education programs are for all students. There are a few programs currently in place that are specifically for the high risk groups. The success of these efforts has not yet been evaluated.

Drug Treatment

The federal government has invested a great deal of money and interest in developing a drug that will reduce cocaine abuse. Such a drug has not yet been identified, but there are several ways in which it might work. The drug could block cocaine's effects altogether, so there would be no high and no craving. There are drugs like this for heroin abuse, and it is difficult to get addicts to take them for long periods of time. A drug could make a user ill each time cocaine is taken. A drug called antabuse or disulfuram works this way with alcohol. Again, alcoholics are reluctant to take it. A third possibility is a drug that can substitute for cocaine but which has milder effects. This would allow users to function better in society. The crime related to cocaine-seeking behavior would be reduced. The disadvantage is that a substitute would still most likely be an addictive drug. Its distribution would have to be controlled. It would also be difficult to get a person off the substitute drug. The drug methadone functions in this way for heroin abusers. It is certainly better than heroin, but it does not solve the drug abuse problem.

While a drug that works specifically on cocaine abuse is being developed, other drug treatments have been tried. They have had only limited success.[11] One type of drug treatment is antidepressant medication. This is based on the idea that many users are taking cocaine to self-medicate for depression. Two studies with the antidepressant medication, desipramine, found that cocaine users had reduced craving and stayed off cocaine longer than those who received an inactive medication (placebo). Others have reported that desipramine can trigger a relapse in patients who have stopped using cocaine.[12] Another study found that desipramine had no effect, but the doses may have been too low. More recently another antidepressant, fluoxetine (Prozac)™, has been tested. Again the results are mixed. One laboratory reported no effect while another is reporting that Prozac™ helps reduce cocaine craving and use.

In a group of heroin users who also happened to use cocaine, some success was recently found with an opioid-type drug (buprenorphine).[13] This drug was being tested for its ability to reduce heroin abuse. It was compared to the standard methadone

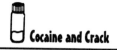

treatment. It was as good as or better than methadone. Unexpectedly, the research group found that cocaine use was reduced in the buprenorphine group. Further studies have confirmed the initial results.

Many of the drug treatments are tested on laboratory animals that have been trained to self-administer cocaine. The drug treatments are much more effective at reducing cocaine consumption in animals than in humans. There may be an obvious reason for this. The environment is very different in the animal cage. There is nothing else to do but take cocaine, and nearly all of the animals exposed to cocaine will take it. Drug treatment interferes with cocaine self-administration in most of the animals. In the human environment most people do not take cocaine. Those that do may be controlled by a special set of environmental conditions that would make them more resistant to treatment. Nevertheless, animal studies are useful for screening what type of treatment drugs may be more effective than others.

Behavioral Treatment

There is a wide array of methods designed to change behavior. Some have been more effective than others in treating cocaine abuse.

Community Reinforcement Approach (CRA). This method has been successfully used in the treatment of alcoholism. Recently it has been used with cocaine addicts in a study at the University of Vermont.[14] The basic idea is to reward cocaine users for staying off cocaine by giving other rewarding events in the community. Eventually addicts are trained to seek pleasure from these other sources of reward rather than from drugs. The way the program works is that a cocaine addict is asked to stop using cocaine. The client is regularly required to come in to the laboratory to give a urine sample. If it is negative, does not show signs of cocaine, the client receives some points. The points can be traded in for specific "prizes." These might be tickets to a game, video rentals, food, or personal care products. The goal is to use the points to purchase something that will improve the person's lifestyle and/or social interactions. It is hoped that participation in other events will compete with cocaine use and will help the individual remain drug free.

Cue Exposure. This treatment method is also relatively new and is based on the idea that getting people off cocaine is not the most difficult part of the problem. The real challenge is preventing them from returning to drug use. This behavior is called relapse. What usually triggers relapse are cues (sights, sounds, people, places, etc.) that were previously associated with drug use. These cues may have two possible effects on the ex-cocaine addict. They may cause intense craving or they may reinitiate some of the other withdrawal effects that were experienced right after cocaine use was stopped. Both of these problems could be solved by relapsing or starting to take the drug again. The cue exposure method trains ex-users to face these cues without getting the urge to take cocaine. This may be done by repeated exposure.[15] Clients are hooked up to electrical devices that monitor their blood pressure and heart rate. At first, cue exposure causes large changes in these measures. After repeated cue exposures they no longer physically react. It is then assumed that the cue has lost its ability to produce relapse.

Another method involves relaxation training. When the cue is presented, the ex-cocaine user performs exercises that

71

will relax him and divert his attention from the cue. Some of the early results from these studies have found that mood is important to the effect of cues and relapse. If the user was most likely to take drugs when in a depressed mood, then cues will be more effective when the depressed mood returns. Hypnosis could be used to recreate that mood, and then cue exposure training could be more effective.

Contingency Contracting. This method was successful among a group of cocaine users made up of doctors, lawyers, or other professionals in Colorado in the 1980s.[16] It has not been tested with low income, inner-city crack users. This form of treatment is relatively harsh. Only half of those entering treatment agreed to try it. The clients were required to write letters to their employers or licensing boards if they were doctors, dentists, or lawyers. The letters stated that they had a problem with cocaine that impaired their ability to perform their jobs. In some cases the letters were written to family members who were unaware of the client's cocaine habit. Urine samples were randomly collected. According to the rules of the contract, the letter would be mailed if the urine was positive for cocaine. It would be kept confidentially on file as long as the urine samples were negative for cocaine. This method successfully kept more than half of a small sample of patients off cocaine for up to a year.

Therapies That Change Thinking and Behavior. These are more traditional methods that involve one or more meetings per week with a therapist. They may be individual or group therapy. The goal is to educate users about the adverse effects of drugs. They are also educated about the pressures exerted by dealers and other users. Training is given about how to resist these pressures. Emphasis is given to resume a healthier lifestyle. Homework assignments are often given, such as participating in activities other than drug taking. Work is done to improve self-esteem and confidence. This type of therapy has not been very successful on its own. However, when it is combined with other approaches such as drug therapy or the community reinforcement approach, the combination is more successful than either method alone.

Therapeutic Communities. This method is similar to the therapies that change thinking and behavior. There are seminars and counseling. The difference is that the patients live in the treatment facility, usually for at least six months. Most of the staff are former addicts. The real value of a therapeutic community is that it keeps the user away from a familiar environment and peers that may trigger relapse. It allows them to develop a drug-free lifestyle among people who have the same goal. Studies of the effectiveness of treatment communities indicate that those who stay for ninety days or more are less likely to go back to daily drug use than untreated groups. Therapeutic communities mainly consist of male residents. In some communities there are males and females, but females do not do as well as males in mixed groups. There are only a few therapeutic communities for women only; more are badly needed.

12-step Programs. Programs like Cocaine Anonymous (CA), Alcoholics Anonymous (AA), or Narcotics Anonymous (NA), are successful and important forms of treatment. They all have the goal of helping participants to be totally drug-free. They assume that the addiction is a disease that has to be managed from day to day. The 12 steps require the addict to admit they have no control over drug-taking. They turn their will over to God or a higher power. They pledge to make amends to those who were harmed by their addiction. Finally, they promise to carry the message of spiritual awakening to other drug abusers. The value of 12-step programs is that they are easily accessible and free. They use a buddy system so that members can encourage each other to remain drug-free for a long period of time. This program is often recommended in combination with many of the other treatments. It is difficult to conduct a scientific evaluation of this method, because members come and go at irregular intervals and they choose to remain anonymous.[17] Most residential and outpatient treatment programs incorporate the 12-step process into their therapy session.

Questions for Discussion

1. Does education prevent cocaine abuse?

2. What is the best method of preventing drug abuse?

3. What is the best method of stopping cocaine abuse?

5

Personal Aspects of Cocaine Abuse

Currently, in the United States, approximately 15 percent of high school seniors, 21 percent of college students, and 30 percent of young adults have tried cocaine.[1] Cocaine use is increasing faster among women then men. The highest rates of cocaine use are among eighteen- to twenty-five-year-olds and the unemployed. Among those who are between twenty and forty years old, cocaine use in the unemployed is double that of the employed. Cocaine use affects all North American youth regardless of age, gender, ethnic background, culture, race, education, or socioeconomic status. Cocaine abuse is experienced by rural as well as urban and suburban youth, although use is higher in the large cities and in the western United States.

Who is Most Likely to Use Cocaine?

There is no single cause of cocaine abuse that could clearly identify who is most likely to use it. Cocaine abuse is influenced by

Who Inner City Teens (ages 12-19) Talk to About Drugs

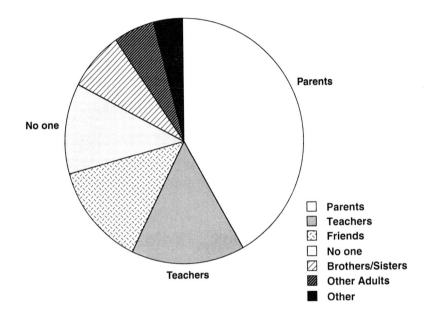

A national survey in Atlanta of inner-city teens between the ages of twelve and nineteen shows that teens talk to their families most about drugs and drug-related problems.

many factors relating to the individual, such as heredity and personality. It is also determined by many environmental factors like neighborhoods and friends. There are also protective factors that may cancel out some of the risk factors. A protective factor might be doing very well at school or having an extremely supportive parent. There is no simple path or combination of factors that can strongly predict who will use cocaine. However, the more risk factors a person has and the fewer protective factors there are, the more likely drug use will occur.

Most experts agree on the many risk factors that are related to drug abuse. However, there may be some exceptions. Some risk factors are specific to certain drugs, like genetics and alcohol. Also, certain subgroups of the population, such as inner-city African Americans may have special risk factors that are tied to their specific culture. For instance, many of these youth live in predominantly single parent homes where there is added pressure to support the family. Some of the risk factors that experts agree on are listed on the following pages under personal, environmental, and familial factors. Many of the risk factors actually fit in more than one category. Almost everyone has some of these risk factors. Again, the key point is that potential cocaine abusers have many of them.

An additional factor is simply drug use. Occasional drug use can lead to drug abuse. Cocaine-abusing teens are more likely to have used drugs early and used large amounts. Drugs like cocaine are initially used for reasons such as ignorance, curiosity, boredom, thrill-seeking, and escape from peer pressure. Later they are used more frequently to help lessen the pain of problems like those listed in the following charts.

Personality

- Childhood behavior/conduct problems.

- Aggressive, acting-out behavior.

- Impulsive behavior.

- Hyperactivity/attention deficit disorder.

- Difficulties in coping with peer pressure.

- Social isolation.

- Traumatic experiences (murders, deaths, other losses).

- Victim of physical abuse.

- Victim of sexual abuse.

- Poor school performance.

- Inadequate feeling of being loved.

- Negative feelings (depression).

- Inability to experience pleasure.

Environment

- Easy availability of drug.

- Low cost of drug.

- Many drug-using peers.

- Low-income, crowded, inner-city location.

- Individual is not part of the local religious community.

Family

- Parents abuse drugs.

- Parents are alcoholics.

- Psychiatric disorders in parents (depression, antisocial).

- Family disruption—divorce.

- Legal problems—deviant behavior in parents.

Are Certain Personalities More Likely to Use Cocaine?

Drug users are often described by one or more personality types.[2] For instance, cocaine users are often described as impulsive. This means that they act quickly before thinking about the consequences. They want things immediately. An impulsive person would quickly spend his allowance on something he did not need instead of saving for something that may be important to him later.

Cocaine users can also be described as risk-takers. These are people who get a thrill from taking a chance on something that could be harmful. It may be a drug such as cocaine. Some risk-takers like drugs such as LSD or PCP because they never have the same trip twice. It may be a good or bad trip, but what interests this type of person is that the outcome cannot be predicted. Risk-takers may seek out other activities such as skydiving or bungee jumping. The economic situation and the environment may determine whether they will choose a drug or another activity for risk-taking.

Low self-esteem is a personality factor that seems to be related to cocaine use. This means that people have feelings of low self-worth. They do not believe that they are much good at things or have much value to other people. They may often feel frustrated, defeated, and that they are not as good as other people. Drugs such as cocaine give them a false sense of importance or power that temporarily puts aside their low self-image.

Depression and anxiety are other conditions that can lead to cocaine use. Depression is a constant feeling of sadness, fatigue, and inability to enjoy activities that are normally pleasurable. Anxiety is excessive worry and concern about past, current, and future events. These conditions are rare in children, but they become more common in teens. They are very common in adults. It is thought that they might be due to a chemical imbalance in the brain because drugs that successfully treat these conditions change brain chemistry. Unfortunately, cocaine may change the brain's chemical imbalance in the same way, giving users relief from depression or anxiety. These conditions would be better treated under a doctor's supervision with nonaddictive and safer medications.

Another personality feature that is related to cocaine use is a person's religious beliefs or the strength of his societal values. Values that instruct a person not to harm himself or others are formed in early childhood with the help of family and society. They help prevent drug addiction. If you never learn moral and

81

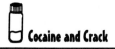

ethical values, you will not be able to see the damage you are doing to yourself and others when you do drugs.

A Personal Story

This is a true story of a teenage girl who came from an inner-city home where her father left home and her mother had to raise several children on her own. Her mother used alcohol and marijuana. When Ann was thirteen she left home and stayed in foster homes. She felt that her mother treated her like a slave, and she was tired of being beaten. Ann began using alcohol and marijuana around the time she left home. She quit school in the tenth grade and began to live with a series of boyfriends. That is when her crack use began. For the next five or six years, she lived on the streets. She got money for her crack habit from drug dealing in partnership with boyfriends and their families. She also relied on prostitution and theft. Ann used cocaine every day for five or six years. She usually started in the morning, and continued into the early afternoon. She tried to stop long enough each day to eat lunch and get some sleep in the late afternoon. She estimated that her cocaine habit cost between five and ten thousand dollars each month. Ann is now twenty-two. She is homeless but sometimes stays with relatives. She has never married. She has been pregnant six times. She has four children, one on the way, and one who died prematurely. She used crack heavily during all of these pregnancies. Her four children are in foster care. She hopes to keep the one she is expecting by entering a residential treatment facility for women and their children. Ann has been through treatment for her cocaine habit ten times. She has been hospitalized twice for depression. She is currently in treatment and is receiving medication for depression. Her dream is to get off cocaine for good, to get a job, and to be able to live with all of her children. Ann hopes to resolve her legal problems. She has a number of bench warrants and parole violations. She may need to spend some time in jail or earn money to pay fines before her legal problems are settled.[3]

Questions for Discussion

1. Is there an addictive personality?

2. Can special efforts prevent cocaine abuse in high-risk children?

3. What are some characteristics of the family and environment that may be related to cocaine abuse?

6

The Family's Role

Is Vulnerability to Cocaine Abuse Inherited From Parents?

Family studies have been conducted to examine this question. This type of study is very difficult to do. Families share genes which may control drug addiction. But they also share environments, cultures, diets, and major life events, and there are many paths to cocaine addiction.[1] To study the contribution of purely genetic factors versus the shared environment, twin studies have been done.[2] Most of these studies have dealt with alcoholism. Identical twins who share all the same genes can be compared to nonidentical twins who share only half of their genes. If the identical twin pairs are both more likely to be drug abusers than the nonidentical pair, then part of the drug abuse is explained by genetics. Another type of study is the twin adoption study. Identical twins who were separated and adopted at birth are compared to identical twins that were raised in the same family. For a time in England, for economic reasons, parents gave up

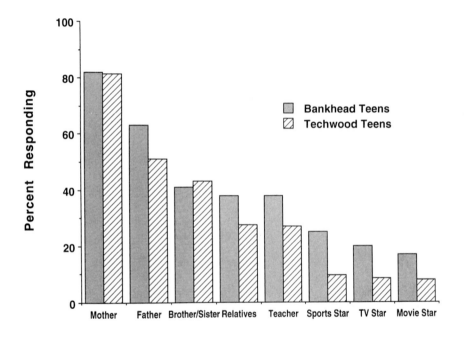

Who 12-19 year old teens look up to

A national survey of inner-city teens between the ages of twelve and nineteen from two Atlanta communities shows that family members and teachers are the ones that teens most look up to.

one identical twin for adoption. If genes determine drug abuse, it should not matter that some twins were raised in a different environment; all twin pairs should be similar. If one twin abuses drugs, the other twin abuses drugs. If environment is more important, there should be less agreement on drug addiction in the identical twins that were raised apart.

The results of studies such as these show that family transmission or genetic factors explains about 30 percent of alcoholism. The remaining 70 percent is explained by the environment.[3] Thus, the environment has the overwhelming influence. There have not yet been as many twin studies of other abused drugs such as cocaine, heroin, or marijuana. Results of these few studies suggest that there is much less transmission of the addictive behavior due to genes. With both alcohol and other drugs, there is a slightly stronger genetic effect in men.[4]

In summary, very little of cocaine abuse is truly passed on through your parents' genes and present at birth. If it seems that cocaine abuse is inherited, it is because the environment has risk factors and both parent and child live in the same environment. Actually, one of the strongest influences on teenage drug abuse is having friends who use drugs.[5] Your parents also serve as role models. It is difficult to determine what is due to inheritance and what is due to behavioral modeling. Overall, prevention and treatment efforts have to work with either changing the environment or making young people more resistant to negative environmental influences.

The Family's Attitude About Cocaine

Support groups consisting of family and friends help teens stay away from drugs. These groups can be extended families, parents, siblings, grandparents, and other family members, or they can consist of young people from a church or after-school organization. If there is cocaine or other drug abuse in your family, it puts you at high risk. There are two ways to reduce that risk. One is to form a close relationship with an older member of the community of the same gender and ethnic background who does not use drugs. This person could serve as a role model in place of an older sibling or parent. Second, you could get involved in activities during and after school that are pleasurable and rewarding in place of using drugs.

Questions for Discussion

1. Do you think there is a chance of preventing cocaine abuse in teens who have one or more addicted parents?

2. How can a family help prevent cocaine abuse?

7

Where to Go For Help

Where to Turn if You Need Help

There are several options if you need help. One important tip to remember is that sooner is better. Most treatments work better before drug abuse has become very heavy and long term. Another point is that it is possible to get help within the community without all your friends and relatives knowing about the problem. Treatment programs are very careful about confidentiality.

The first place to start is locally. A guidance counselor at school may help. Boy's or Girl's Clubs and the YMCA are trained to help direct you to treatment programs. If you belong to a religious organization, the pastor, priest, or rabbi in charge of the youth programs will be helpful. If your family has health insurance or belongs to a health maintenance organization, there are programs available for teen drug users. Most of the big hospitals in town have treatment programs. The best approach would be to learn about several programs that are available locally and decide which one you would feel most comfortable with.

CSAP's Regional Alcohol and Drug Awareness Resource (RADAR) Network consists of state clearinghouses, specialized information centers of national organizations, and the Department of Education Regional Training Centers. Each RADAR Network member can offer the public a variety of information services. Check with the representative in your area to find out what services are available.

CSAP'S (Center for Substance Abuse Prevention) Radar Network State Centers

*Indicates membership on Steering Committee

Alabama
Crystal Jackson
Division of Substance
Abuse Services
Alabama Department of Mental
Health/Mental Retardation
200 Interstate Park Drive
P.O. Box 3710
Montgomery, AL 36193
(205) 270-4640

Alaska
Joyce Paulus
Alaska Council on Prevention of
Alcohol and Drug Abuse
3333 Denali Street
Suite 201
Anchorage, AK 99503
(907) 258-6021

American Samoa
Faimafilioalii Taamu
Department of
Human Resources
Social Services Division
Alcohol and Drug Program
Government of
American Samoa
Pago Pago, AS 96799
(684) 633-4485
Fax: (684) 633-1139

Arizona
Nancy Hanson
Arizona Prevention
Resource Center
Arizona State University
College of Extended Education
Tempe, AZ 85287-1708
(602) 965-9666
Fax: (602) 965-8198

Arkansas

Percy Brown
Office of Alcohol and Drug
Abuse Prevention
400 Donaghey Plaza North
7th and Main Street
Little Rock, AR 72203-1437
(501) 682-6656

*California

Peggy Blair
State of California
Department of Alcohol
and Drug Programs
4th Floor
1700 K Street
Sacramento, CA 95814-4022
(916) 327-8447

Colorado

Linda Garrett
Colorado Alcohol &
Drug Abuse Division
Resource Department
4300 Cherry Creek Drive
South Denver, CO 80220-1530
(303) 692-2930
(303) 692-2956
Fax: (303) 782-4883

Connecticut

Kathleen Senese
Connecticut Clearinghouse
334 Farmington Avenue
Plainville, CT 06062
(203) 793-9791
(203) 793-9813

Delaware

Sheri P. Russel
Office of Prevention Resource
Clearinghouse
Delaware Youth and
Family Center
1825 Faulkland Road
Wilmington, DE 19805-1195
(302) 633-2704
Fax: (302) 633-2565

District of Columbia

Mary Ivey
Office of Health Planning and
Development
1660 L Street, N.W.
Suite 1117
Washington, DC 20036
(202) 673-7481
Fax: (202) 727-2386

Florida

Cindy Colvin
Florida Alcohol and
Drug Abuse Association
1030 E. Lafayette
Suite 100
Tallahassee, FL 32301-4547
(904) 878-6922
(904) 878-2196
Fax: (904) 878-6584

Georgia

Marie Albert
Georgia Prevention
Resource Center
Division of Mental Health
Room 319
878 Peachtree Street, N.E.
Atlanta, GA 30309
(404) 894-4204

Guam

Richard Colamba
Department of Mental Health
and Substance Abuse
P.O. Box 9400
Tamuning, GU 96911
(671) 646-9261
(671) 646-9269
Fax: (671) 649-6948

Hawaii

Timothy Smith
Drug Free Hawaii
Prevention Resource Center
1218 Waimanu Street
Honolulu, HI 96814
(808) 524-5509
(808) 524-0570

Idaho

Phyllis Sawyer
Boise State University
Idaho Radar Network Center
1910 University Drive
Boise, ID 83725
(208) 385-3471
Fax: (208) 385-3334

**Illinois*

Caroline Murphy/
George Dirks
Prevention Resource
Center Library
822 S. College
Springfield, IL 62704
(217) 525-3456
Fax: (217) 789-4388

Indiana

Barbara Seitz
Indiana University
Indiana Prevention
Resource Center
Room 110
840 State Road, 46 Bypass
Bloomington, IN 47405
(812) 855-1237
(812) 855-4940

**Iowa*

Tressa Youngbear
Iowa Substance Abuse
Information Center
Cedar Rapids Public Library
500 1st Street, S.E.
Cedar Rapids, IA 52401
(319) 398-5133
Fax: (319) 398-0408

Kansas

Judy Donovan
Kansas Alcohol and Drug
Abuse Services
Department of Social
and Rehabilitation Services
300 S.W. Oakley
Topeka, KS 66606
(913) 296-3925
Fax: (913) 296-0511

*Maine

Earle Simpson, Jr.
Office of Substance
Abuse Clearinghouse
State House Station #159
24 Stone Street
Augusta, ME 04333
(207) 287-2962

Kentucky

Dianne D. Shuntich
Drug Information
Services
for Kentucky
Division of Substance Abuse
275 E. Main Street
Frankfort, KY 40621
(502) 564-2880

*Maryland

Standola Reynolds
Alcohol and Drug
Abuse Administration
Department of Health
and Mental Hygiene, 4th Floor
201 W. Preston Street
Baltimore, MD 21201
(410) 225-6914
Fax: (410) 333-7206

Louisiana

Sanford W. Hawkins, Sr.
Division of Alcohol and
Drug Abuse
P.O. Box 3868
1201 Capitol Access Road
Baton Rouge, LA 70821-3868
(504) 342-9352
Fax: (504) 342-1384

Massachusetts

Janet Shea
The Psychological Center's
Prevention Network
488 Essex Street
Lawrence, MA 01840
(508) 688-2323
Fax: (508) 681-1281

Michigan

Gail Johnsen
Michigan Substance Abuse
and Traffic Safety
Information Center
2409 E. Michigan
Lansing, MI 48912-4019
(517) 482-9902
Fax: (517) 482-8262

Minnesota

Mary Scheide
Minnesota Prevention
Resource Center
417 University Avenue
St. Paul, MN 55103-1995
(612) 224-5121
(800) 223-5833

Mississippi

Anne Goforth
Mississippi Department
of Mental Health
Division of Alcoholism
and Drug Abuse
1101 Robert E. Lee Building,
9th Floor
239 N. Lamar Street
Jackson, MS 39207
(601) 359-1288

Missouri

Randy Smith/Jeanne Massic
Missouri Division of Alcohol
and Drug Abuse
1706 E. Elm Street
Jefferson City, MO 65102
(314) 751-4942
Fax: (314) 751-7814

Montana

Kenneth C. Taylor
Department of Institutions
Chemical Dependency Bureau
1539 11th Avenue
Helena, MT 59620
(406) 444-2878

Nebraska

Karen Weise
Alcoholism and Drug Abuse
Council of Nebraska
650 J Street, Suite 215
Lincoln, NE 68508
(402) 474-0930
(402) 474-1992

Nevada

Marjorie Walker
Bureau of Alcohol
and Drug Abuse
505 E. King Street, Suite 500
Carson City, NV 89710
(702) 687-4790
Fax: (702) 687-5980

New Hampshire
Mary Dube
New Hampshire Office of
Alcohol and Drug Abuse
 Prevention
State Office Park South
105 Pleasant Street
Concord, NH 03301
(603) 271-6100
Fax: (603) 271-5051

New Jersey
Barry Hantman
New Jersey State Department of
Health
Division of Alcoholism
and Drug Abuse
129 E. Hanover Street
Trenton, NJ 08625
(609) 984-6961
Fax: (609) 292-3816

New Mexico
Elaine Benavidez
Department
of Health/BHSD-DSA
1190 St. Francis Drive
Room N3200
Santa Fe, NM 87502-6110
(505) 827-2601
Fax: (505) 827-0097

New York
Leslie S. Connor
New York Division
of Alcoholism and
Alcohol Abuse
194 Washington Avenue
Albany, NY 12210
(518) 474-3460
Fax: (518) 474-3004

Judith M. Lukin
National Development and
Research Institute, Inc.
11 Beach Street, 2nd Floor
New York, NY 10013
(212) 966-8700
Fax: (212) 941-1539

North Carolina
Betty Lane
North Carolina Alcohol and
Drug Resource Center
3109A University Drive
Durham, NC 27707-3703
(919) 493-2881

*North Dakota
Michele Edwards
North Dakota Prevention
Resource Center
1839 E. Capitol Avenue
Bismarck, ND 58501
(701) 224-3603

Ohio
Deborah Chambers
Ohio Department of Alcohol
and Drug Addiction Services
12th Floor
2 Nationwide Plaza
Columbus, OH 43216
(614) 466-6379

Oklahoma
Norma Janssen
Oklahoma State Department of
Mental Health
1200 NE 13th St., 2nd Floor
P.O. Box 53277
Oklahoma City, OK 73117
(405) 271-8755
Fax: (405) 271-7413

*Oregon
Sue Ziglinski
Oregon Drug and Alcohol
Information
2801 N. Gantenbein
Portland, OR 97227
(503) 280-3673
(800) 237-7808
Fax: (503) 280-4621

Pennsylvania
Jessica Van Ord
PENNSAIC
Columbus Square
652 W. 17th Street
Erie, PA 16502
(814) 459-0245
Fax: (814) 453-4714

Puerto Rico
Alma Negron
Department of Anti-Addiction
Services
414 Barbosa Avenue
Apartado 21414
Rio Piedras, PR 00928-1414
(809) 767-5990
(809) 765-5895

Rhode Island
Betty Ann McHugh
Office of Substance Abuse
Division of
Community Development
P.O. Box 20363
Cranston, RI 02920
(401) 464-2380
Fax: (401) 464-2064

*South Carolina
Elizabeth Peters
South Carolina Commission on
Alcohol & Drug Abuse
The Drug Store Information
Clearinghouse
3700 Forest Drive
Suite 300
Columbia, SC 29204
(803) 734-9559

South Dakota
Jeff McDorman
South Dakota Division
Alcohol and Substance Abuse
3800 E. Highway 34
c/o 500 E. Capitol
Pierre, SD 57501-5070
(605) 773-3123
Fax: (605) 773-5483

Tennessee
Sharon Crockett
Tennessee Alcohol and
Drug Association
545 Mainstream Drive
Suite 404
Nashville, TN 37228
(615) 244-7066
Fax: (615) 255-3704

Texas
Maggie Houston
Texas Commission on Alcohol
and Drug Abuse
Resource Center
720 Brozos Street
Suite 307
Austin, TX 78729
(512) 867-8700
Fax: (512) 480-0679

Utah
Sherry Young
Utah State Division
of Substance Abuse, 4th Floor
120 N. 200 West
Salt Lake City, UT 84145-0500
(801) 538-3939

Vermont
Pam Fontaine
Office of Alcohol and Drug
Abuse Programs
103 S. Main Street
Waterbury, VT 05671-1701
(802) 241-2178
Fax: (802) 244-8103

Virginia
Bernice Morgan
Virginia Department of
Mental Health
P.O. Box 1797
Richmond, VA 23214
(804) 371-7564
(804) 371-6179

Virgin Islands
Marcia Jameson/Annette Garcia
Division of Mental Health
#6 & 7 Estate Diamond Ruby
Charles Harwood Hospital
Richmond, St. Croix, VI 00820
(809) 774-7700
Fax: (809) 774-4701

Washington
Mark Parcher
Washington State Substance
Abuse Coalition (WSSAC)
12729 N.E. 20th
Suite 18
Bellevue, WA 98005-1906
(206) 637-7011
Fax: (206) 637-7012

West Virginia
Shirley A. Smith
West Virginia Library
Commission Cultural Center
Charleston, WV 25305
(304) 558-2041
Fax: (304) 348-2044

Wisconsin
Douglas White
Wisconsin Clearinghouse
315 N. Henry Street
Madison, WI 53703
(608) 263-2797
(608) 263-6886
Fax: (608) 262-0123

Wyoming
Linda Klopp
Wyoming Care Program
University of Wyoming
McWhinnie Hall, Room 115
P.O. Box 3374
Laramie, WY 82071-3374
(307) 766-4119

CSAP RADAR Network Specialty Centers with Descriptions and Areas of Expertise

*indicates membership on steering committee

Alabama
Andrew W. Milwid
Benevolent and Protective Order of Elks
RR # 1, Box 62
Jacksons Gap, AL 36861
(205) 825-4690
Distributes print materials for young children through adults. Assists parents of young people in keeping their children drug-free. State chairperson in 50 states with 2,300 locations nationally; distributes 11to12 million pieces of information annually.
Areas of Expertise: Community Mobilization, Substance Abuse, Youth

Arizona
Travis Jackson
Indian Health Service
Colorado River Service
Route 1, Box 12
Parker, AZ 85344
(602) 669-2137
Fax: (602) 669-5450
The Indian Health Service, Colorado River Service Unit provides technical assistance to Indian communities for the development of resources for the prevention, intervention, and treatment of substance abuse. The Indian Health Service houses a resource library which contains numerous research articles and materials on Native American substance abuse issues.
Areas of Expertise: Community Mobilization, Youth, Training

California

Andrea L. Mitchell
Alcohol Research Group Epidemiology and Behavioral Medicine
Institute of Medical Research, San Francisco
2000 Hearst Ave.
Berkeley, CA 92176
(510) 642-5208
Fax: (510) 642-7175
Resource library for studies on use and related problems of AOD, societal responses. Areas of research include AIDS, treatment and warning label effectiveness, homelessness, fetal alcohol syndrome, epidemiology, delinquency, crime, injuries.
Areas of Expertise: Substance Abuse, Research

Ford S. Hatamiya
Multicultural Training Resource Center
1540 Market St., Suite 320
San Francisco, CA 94102
(415) 861-2142
The Multicultural Training Resource Center (MTRC) of San Francisco was established in 1984 as the first national center to provide multicultural and culturally-specific AIDS and substance abuse prevention services. MTRC provides supportive services for multicultural and culturally distinct organizations, and promotes the establishment of cross-cultural links for collaborative community empowerment.
Areas of Expertise: Training, Hispanic, Asian-Pacific

Nancy Kaihatsu
University of California at San Diego
UCSD Extension 0176
9500 Gilman Drive
La Jolla, CA 92093-0176
(619) 534-6331
Fax: (619) 554-0485

Provides prevention skill-building workshops, research and policy conferences, quarterly periodical-*Prevention File*, campus alcohol risk assessment/prevention resource materials for higher education.
Areas of Expertise: Asian and Pacific Islander Americans, Substance Abuse

*Ford Kuramoto
National Asian Pacific American Families Against Substance Abuse, Inc. (NAPAFASA)
420 E. Third St., Suite 909
Los Angeles, CA 90013-1647
(213) 617-8277
Fax: (213) 617-2012
Private, non-profit, national membership organization focused on AOD materials regarding Asian and Pacific Island populations. Some Asian/Pacific Island language materials, videotapes, and publications list available.
Areas of Expertise: Asian and Pacific Islander Americans, Substance Abuse

James Mosher
The Marin Institute Resource Center for the Prevention of Alcohol and Other Drug Problems
24 Belvedere Street
San Rafael, CA 94901
(415) 456-5692
Fax: (415) 456-0491
Focuses on media and policy research and community action in reducing alcohol and other drug problems in society. Concentrates on changing environments that support/glamorize illicit alcohol and drug use. Monitors marketing activities of alcohol.
Areas of Expertise: Media Advocacy, Substance Abuse, Community Action

Canada

Jill Austin
Canadian Centre on Substance Abuse
112 Kent St., Suite 480
Ottawa, Ontario KIP 5P2
Canada
(613) 235-4048
Fax: (613) 235-8108
Contains literature and audio visuals on alcohol and other drug issues, French-language materials, historical temperance collection and museum. Provides Canadian contacts, unique resources.
Areas of Expertise: Canadian Programs and Services, Librarians

Margy Chan
Addiction Research Foundation Library
33 Russell St.
Toronto, Ontario M5S 2S1
Canada
(416) 595-6072
Fax: (416) 595-6036
Consortium of major substance abuse/addiction libraries and documentation centers. Develops inventory of treatment services, prevention programs, and resource materials in Canada. Developing a national bibliographic data base.
Areas of Expertise: Workplace, Youth, Canadian Programs and Services

District of Columbia

*Gloria Martinez
Helen Munoz
COSSMHO-National Coalition of Hispanic Health Services Organization
1501 16th St., N.W.
Washington, DC 20036
(202) 387-5000
Fax: (202) 797-4353

103

Develops new model programs, conducts research and strengthens local infrastructures by working with community organizations to improve health for Hispanic communities in United States and Puerto Rico.

Areas of Expertise: Hispanic, Prevention, Healthcare

Robert Bennett
Americans for the Restitution and Righting Old Wrongs, Inc.
1000 Connecticut Ave., Suite 1206
Washington, DC 20036
(202) 296-0685
Developed six booklets and four posters to provide American Indian communities with practical resources to combat alcohol and drug abuse. These are available from the ERIC document reproduction service. Provides a training program, legislation review, and information for trainers/presenters.

Areas of Expertise: American Indian, Substance Abuse, Training

Ruth Marie Conolly
Inter-American Drug Information System
OAS/IADIS
1889 F Street N.W., 8th Floor
Washington, DC 20006
(202) 458-3809
The Inter-American Drug Control Commission (IADIS) was established in 1987 with the objective of eliminating illicit drug trafficking and drug abuse. The system is composed of a network of libraries and information centers throughout North, Central, and South America. A bibliographic database is under development.

Areas of Expertise: International, Hispanic, Substance Abuse

Jon Dunbar-Cooper
The National Network of Runaway and Youth Services, Inc.
1400 Eye Street, N.W., Suite 330
Washington, DC 20005
(202) 783-7949

Provides a national electronic communications service called YOUTHNET which connects youth-service professionals across the country. This service provides information on runaway, homeless, and other high risk youth. The Network also has trainers' manuals on safe choices.
Areas of Expertise: Youth, Runaways, HIV/AIDS

Jill Hereford
Resource Center on Substance Abuse Prevention and Disability
1331 F Street, N.W., Suite 800
Washington, DC 20004
(202) 783-2900
Fax: (202) 623-3812
Develops commercial products and services for teachers, parents, and others working with disabled. Raises public awareness about appropriate AOD substance abuse for disabled. Provides personalized attention, literature searches, has reading room.
Areas of Expertise: Substance Abuse, Disability

Georgia
*Beverly E. Allen
Multi-Media Center
720 Westview Dr., S.W.
Atlanta, GA 30310-1495
(404)752-1530
Fax: (404) 755-7318
Contains open stock collection of medical books, monographs, journals, computer-assisted instruction programs, and AV materials. Access via automated library information system. Specializes in Black health issues, AIDS, hypertension, alcohol abuse.
Areas of Expertise: African Americans, Healthcare, Training

105

*Paula Kemp
National Drug Information Center for Families in Action
2296 Henderson Mill Rd., Suite 300
Atlanta, GA 30345
(404) 934-6364
Fax: (404) 934-7137
Houses a collection of 500,000 documents on ATOD issues. Can assist in organizing community prevention groups and translating complex information for the general public. Publishes drug-education curriculum and quarterly drug abuse updates.
Areas of Expertise: Community Mobilization, Policy, Public Housing

Maryland

Lenore Burts
CDC's National AID's Information Clearinghouse
PO Box 6003
Rockville, MD 20850
(800) 458-5231
Works in partnership to develop and deliver HIV-prevention programs and services. Maintains various data bases. Resources include print and AV materials on AIDS/HIV-related illnesses and workplace-related issues. Computerized information network.
Areas of Expertise: AIDS/HIV, Workplace, Prevention

Candi Byrne
Drugs and Crime Data Center and Clearinghouse
1600 Research Blvd.
Rockville, MD 20850
(800) 666-3332
Specializes in collection and distribution of data on drugs and crime. Resources available: information specialists, database, state-specific data, Justice Department statistics and publications, national report on drugs and crime data summaries.
Areas of Expertise: Drugs and Crime, Statistics, Crime/Violence

Sue Ellen Hersh
Residents Initiatives Drug Information and Strategy Clearinghouse
P.O. Box 6424
Rockville, MD 20850
(301) 251-5546
(800) 251-2691
Provides information pertaining to drug use elimination within public and American Indian housing. DISC offers a collection of current information through publications, documents, newsletters. Info specialists assist in making referrals, technical grants.
Areas of Expertise: Substance Abuse, Public Housing, American Indian

Massachusetts
Chris Carter/David Rosenbloom
Join Together—A National Resource for Communities Fighting Substance Abuse
441 Stuart St., Sixth Floor
Boston, MA 02116
(617) 437-1500
A national program helping communities fight substance abuse; includes a computer network, national fellows program, and policy panels. Provides communications strategies to encourage public awareness and help coalitions create media advocacy programs.
Areas of Expertise: Substance Abuse, Media Advocacy, Community Mobilization

Minnesota
*David Grant
Institute on Black Chemical Abuse Resource Center
2616 Nicollet Ave. South
Minneapolis, MN 55407
(612) 871-7878
Fax: (612) 871-2567

Provides resources in prevention, training, and treatment specifically geared to African-American community. Library collection features large number of articles culled from scholarly journals, popular magazines and a variety of chemical dependency publications.
Areas of Expertise: Prevention, Statistics, Media Advocacy

Missouri
Susan Reineke
TARGET
11724 Plaza Circle
P.O. Box 20626
Kansas City, MO 64195
(816) 366-6667
(800) 464-5400
Fax: (816) 464-5571
Provides education/prevention materials on steroids and other performance enhancing drugs. Audience includes K-12 school personnel, students, parents, community leaders. Also provides information/services on ATOD abuse.
Areas of Expertise: Steroids, Youth, Education

New Hampshire
Jean Kinney
Project Cork Institute
Dartmouth University
9 Maynard Street
Hanover, NH 03755-3851
(603) 650-1809
Fax: (603) 650-1614
Provides curricula and training materials, academic support services and consultation, and specialized technical assistance in alcohol and substance abuse fields. Contains information from biological, health, and social sciences in data base form.
Area of Expertise: Substance Abuse, Healthcare, Medical Education

New Jersey

Cathy Weglarz
Center for Alcohol Studies
Rutgers University
Smithers Hall Busch Campus
Piscataway, NJ 08855-0969
(908) 932-4442
Provides reference assistance and interlibrary loans for materials dealing with all aspects of alcohol use and abuse. Telephone and E-mail delivery. Research level collection. Full-text reprints available.
Areas of Expertise: Alcohol, Research, College/University

New York

Jeff Hon
National Council on Alcoholism and Drug Dependence, Inc. (NCADD)
12 West 21st St.
New York, NY 10010
(212) 206-6670
Founded in 1944, provides education about alcoholism and other drug addictions as treatable diseases. Two hundred state and local affiliates. Dispenses medical and scientific information, answers questions, provides publications, and makes referrals to youth.
Areas of Expertise: Youth, Substance Abuse

Jose Luis Rodriguez
Hispanic Information and Telecommunication Network
449 Broadway, 3rd Floor
New York, NY 10013
(212) 966-5660
Fax: (212) 966-5725
Provides educational-oriented, instructional and cultural programming geared to Hispanics. Provides video and teleconferencing services and distance learning programming directed toward Hispanic/Latino audiences.
Area of Expertise: Hispanics

Pennsylvania
Penny Howe
Chemical People Institute
1 Allegheny Square, Suite 720
Pittsburgh, PA 15212
(413) 322-0900
Promotes community task-force model and provides community outreach education through research and use of existing community resources. Can advise on media campaigns, prevention events, community mobilization, and seminars.
Areas of Expertise: Substance Abuse, Statistics, Training

Puerto Rico
Lic, Zoraida Buxo
Asesor del Gobernador
Commonwealth of Puerto Rico
La Forteleza
San Juan, PR 00901
(809) 721-3343
Fax: (809) 721-8589
Serves as contact with Puerto Rican organizations providing substance abuse prevention services, AIDS/HIV information treatment and services, as well as drug trafficking interdiction.
Areas of Expertise: Drugs and Crime, Substance Abuse, HIV/AIDS

Texas
Dr. Geraldo De Cosio
U.S. Mexico Border Health Association
El Paso Field Office/U.S.-Mexico Border
6006 North Mesa, Suite 600
El Paso, TX 79912
(915) 581-6645
Fax: (915) 833-4768
Promotes public and individual health along the U.S./Mexico border by means of reciprocal technical cooperation. Has five bilingual (Spanish/English) publications: *Border Health, Border*

Epidemiological Bulletin, MCH Newsletter, NEWS, and *Annual Report.* Three of these publications have sections that share news on RADAR Network services/information.

Areas of Expertise: Hispanics, HIV/AIDS, Healthcare, Statistics

Virginia

David S. Anderson
Center for Health Promotion
George Mason University
Module G
4400 University Drive
Fairfax, VA 22030
(703) 993-3697
Fax: (703) 237-3216

Voluntary service organization has general referral resources about campus policies, programs, and research available in survey form, and compilation of initiatives.

Areas of Expertise: Youth, Training, College/University

Kathy Gross
Employee Assistance Professionals, Inc. (EAP)
4601 N. Fairfax Dr.
Suite 1001
Arlington, VA 22203
(703) 522-6272
Fax: (703) 522-4585

Provides information by telephone consultation, referrals to authorities, and written sources on employee assistance programs, drugs in the workplace, and other related issues. Publications distributed by EAP include standards, guidelines, and directories.

Area of Expertise: Workplace

Gregory R. Somavia
CSAP National Resource Center for the Prevention of Perinatal Abuse of Alcohol and Other Drugs
9300 Lee Highway

Fairfax, VA 22031
(703) 218-5600/80
Fax: (703) 218-5701
Provides technical assistance, special training, and information services related to perinatal prevention to professionals in the field. Addresses ATOD abuse among women, their infants and families.
Areas of Expertise: Training, Substance Abuse, Pregnancy

Washington
Nancy Sutherland
University of Washington Alcoholism and
Drug Abuse Institute Library
3937 15th Ave., N.E.
N1-15
Seattle, WA 98105
(206) 543-0937
Fax: (206) 543-5473
Research includes alcoholism and sexual violence, sexual risk-taking, drinking and driving, and treatment matching. Provides database, bibliography, searches. Modest fees charged for outside-state searches; copies done as time permits.
Areas of Expertise: College/University, Research, Substance Abuse

Wisconsin
Doug Stevens/Paul Mladnick
National Rural Institute on Alcohol and Drug Abuse
Arts and Sciences Outreach Office
University of Wisconsin-Eau Claire
Eau Claire, WI 54702-4004
(715) 836-2031
Offers a variety of information, training, and consultation pertaining to rural substance abuse, clinical and programmatic issues. Specializes in substance abuse in topic areas specifically targeted to rural communities.
Areas of Expertise: Rural, Healthcare, Impaired Driving

Department of Education Regional Training Centers

The Regional Training Centers provide training assistance and expertise to local schools to prevent and reduce alcohol and other drug use by students.

Illinois
Donna Wagner
Midwest Regional Center for Drug-Free Schools and Communities
1990 Spring Rd., 3rd Floor
Oakbrook, IL 60521
(708) 571-4710
Provides training, technical assistance, planning and information resources to support schools and communities in ten Midwestern States to combat use of alcohol and other drugs by children and adolescents.
Areas of Expertise: Youth, Training, Community Mobilization

Kentucky
Mary Jane Aboud
Southeast Regional Center for Drug-Free
Schools and Communities
Speceriran Office Plaza
Suite 350
University of Louisville
Louisville, KY 40292
(502) 588-0052
Serves ten states, Puerto Rico, and U.S. Virgin Islands. Has full-time field coordinators in each area to develop prevention plans tailored to area's particular needs. Provides training and technical assistance to school/community teams.
Areas of Expertise: Youth, Training, Community Mobilization

New York
Larry McCullough
Evaluation and Dissemination/

113

Northeast Regional Center for Drug-Free
Schools and Communities
12 Overtone Avenue
Sayville, NY 11782
Assists schools and communities in northeast region develop viable
prevention and early intervention programs. Provides training,
technical assistance to school districts in AOD prevention and
education programs.
Areas of Expertise: Youth, Training, Community Mobilization

Oklahoma
Margretta Bartlett
Southwest Regional Center for Drug-Free Schools and
Communities
University of Oklahoma
555 Constitution Avenue
Norman, OK 73037
In its role as a catalyst, works to build the capacities of schools,
communities, service providers and policy-makers through training
activities, and regional and state-specific events. Provides print
materials, training modules, and an online computer service.
Areas of Expertise: Youth, Training, Community Mobilization

Oregon
Kathy Laws
Western Center for Drug-Free Schools and Communities
Northwest Regional Education Laboratory
101 S.W. Main Street
Suite 500
Portland, OR 97204-3212
(503) 275-9500
Provides prevention and intervention strategies through training,
technical assistance, and information resources to school personnel,
community organizations and parent groups to help organize
effective alcohol and drug abuse prevention programs.
Areas of Expertise: Youth, Training, Community Mobilization

Chapter Notes

Chapter 1

1. R.C. Peterson, "Cocaine: An Overview." Peterson, R.C. and Stillman, R. (Eds) *Cocaine:* 1977, National Institute on Drug Abuse Monograph No. 13. U.S. Government Printing Office: Washington, D.C., 1977, pp. 17–28.

2. R. Ashley, *Cocaine: Its History and Effects.* New York: Warner Books, 1976.

3. R.E. Schultes, "Coca in the Northwest Amazon." *Journal of Ethnopharmacology.* 3: 1981, pp. 173–194.

4. J. Kennedy, *Coca Exotica: The Illustrated Story of Cocaine.* Rutherford, N.J.: Fairleigh Dickinson University Press, 1985.

5. Peterson, R.C., pp. 17-28.

6. C.E. Johanson and M.W. Fischman, "The Pharmacology of Cocaine Related to Its Abuse." *Pharmacological Reviews.* 41: 1989, pp. 3–52.

7. R. Byck, *Cocaine papers: Sigmund Freud.* New York: Stonehill Publishing Co., 1974.

8. Ibid.

9. B. Holmstedt, "Historical Survey." Efron, D.H. (Ed.) *Ethnopharmacological Search For Psychoactive Drugs.* U.S. Public Health Service Publication No. 1645, U.S. Government Printing Office, Washington, D.C., 1967. pamphlet.

10. D.F. Musto, "Opium, Cocaine and Marijuana in American History." *Scientific American.* July 1991, p. 40.

11. Peterson, R.C., p. 31.

12. A.C. Doyle, "The Sign of the Four." *The Complete Sherlock Holmes,* New York: Garden City Publishing, 1938.

Chapter 2

1. P.T. White, "Coca—An Ancient Herb Turns Deadly." *National Geographic.* 175: 1989, p. 3.

2. E.A. Warner, "Cocaine Abuse." *Annals of Internal Medicine.* 119: 1993, pp. 226–235.

3. R.C. Peterson, "Cocaine: An Overview." Peterson, R.C. and Stillman, R.C. (Eds) *Cocaine:* 1977, National Institute on Drug Abuse Monograph No. 13. U.S. Government Printing Office: Washington, D.C., 1977, pp. 17–28.

4. C.E. Johanson and M.W. Fischman, "The Pharmacology of Cocaine Related to Its Abuse." *Pharmacological Reviews.* 41: 1989, pp. 3–52.

5. M. Stone, "Coke Inc. Inside the Big Business of Drugs." *New York.* July 16, 1990, pp. 20–29.

6. G. Witkin, "The Men Who Created Crack." *U.S. News & World Report.* August 19, 1991, pp. 44–53.

7. National Institute on Drug Abuse, "National Household Survey on Drug Abuse: Main Findings," 1990. U.S. Department of Health and Human Services: Washington, D.C., Publication number (ADM) 91-1732, 1991. pamphlet.

8. L.A. Pagliaro and A.M. Pagliaro, "The Phenomenon of Abusable Psychotropic Use Among North American Youth." *Journal of Clinical Pharmacology.* 33: 1993, pp. 676–690.

9. D. Musto, "A Brief History of American Drug Control." *OAH Magazine of History.* Fall 1991. pamphlet

10. G.R. Gay, D.S. Inaba, C.W. Sheppard, and J.A. Newmyer. "Cocaine: History, Epidemiology, Human Pharmacology and Treatment. A Perspective on a New Debut for an Old Girl." *Clinical Toxicology.* 8: 1975, pp. 149–178.

11. P.B. Barash, "Cocaine in Clinical Medicine." *Cocaine:* 1977, Peterson, R.C. and Stillman, R.C. (Eds.). NIDA Research Monograph #13, U.S. Government Printing Office: Washington, D.C., 1977, pp. 193–201.

12. American Medical Association. Department of Drugs. Local Anesthetics. In AMA Drug Evaluations (2nd Ed.). Actors, MD, Publishing Sciences Group, 1973, pp. 212–213.

13. D.R. Wesson and D.E. Smith, "Cocaine: Its Use for Central Nervous System Stimulation Including Recreational and Medical Uses." *Cocaine:* 1977, Peterson, R.C. and Stillman, R.C. (Eds.). NIDA Research Monograph #13, U.S. Government Printing Office: Washington, D.C., 1977, pp. 137–152.

14. L. Grinspoon and J.B. Bakalar, "Coca and Cocaine As Medicines: An Historical Review." *Journal of Ethnopharmacology.* 3: 1981, pp. 149–159.

Chapter 3

1. N.L. Benowitz, "Clinical Pharmacology and Toxicology of Cocaine." *Pharmacology Toxicology.* 72: 1993, pp. 3–12.

2. J.H. Jaffe, N.G. Cascella, K.M. Kumor, and M.A. Sherer, "Cocaine-induced Cocaine Craving." *Psychopharmacology.* 97: 1989, pp. 59–64.

3. K.T. Brady, et al. "Cocaine-induced Psychosis." *Journal of Clinical Psychiatry.* 52: 1991, p. 509.

4. C.E. Johanson and M.W. Fischman, "The Pharmacology of Cocaine Related to Its Abuse." *Pharmacological Reviews.* 41: 1989, pp. 3–52.

5. K. Tardiff, E. Gross, J. Wu, M. Stajic, and R. Millman, "Analysis of Cocaine Positive Fatalities." *Journal of Forensic Science.* 34: pp. 53–63.

6. P.J. Goldstein, H.H. Brownstein, P.J. Ryan, and P.A. Bellucci, "Most Drug-Related Murders Result From Crack Sales, Not Use." *Drug Policy Lett.* March-April 1990, pp. 6–9.

7. A. Licata, S. Taylor, M. Berman, and J. Cranston, "Effects of Cocaine on Human Aggression." *Pharmacology, Biochemistry and Behavior.* 45: 1992, pp. 549–552.

8. A.W. Fischman, C.R. Schuster, and S. Rajfer, "A Comparison of the Subjective and Cardiovascular Effects of Cocaine and Procaine in Humans." *Pharmacology, Biochemistry and Behavior.* 18: 1983, pp. 711–716, .

9. C. Van Dyke, P. Jaltow, J. Ungerer, P.G. Barash, and R. Byck, "Oral Cocaine: Plasma Concentrations and Central Effects." *Science.* 200: 1978, pp. 211–213.

10. The use of human subjects must be approved by a committee at each research institution. Human subjects for studies on drugs of abuse are approved only for subjects who are regular users of the drug and for those who use quantities that are greater than the amount that will be used in the study. If a very limited exposure to the drug is to be given, approval may be obtained for drug naive users, but only for drugs that do not have a high potential for abuse or toxicity.

11. D.C.S. Roberts, E.A. Loh, and G. Vickers, "Self-administration of Cocaine on a Progressive Ratio Schedule in Rate: Dose-response Relationship and the Effect of Haloperidol Pretreatment." *Psychopharmacology.* 97, 1989: pp. 535–538.

12. M.E. Carroll and S.T. Lac, "Autoshaping IV Cocaine Self-administration in Rats: Effects of Nondrug Alternative Reinforcers on Acquisition." *Psychopharmacology.* 110: 1993, pp. 5–12 .

13. T.G. Aigner and R.L. Balster, "Choice Behavior in Rhesus Monkeys: Cocaine Versus Food." *Science.* 210: 1978, pp. 534–535.

14. E.A. Warner, "Cocaine Abuse." *Annals of Internal Medicine.* 119: 1993, pp. 226–235.

15. J. Berry, "Neuropsychological Deficits in Abstinent Cocaine Abusers: Preliminary Findings After Two Weeks of Abstinence." *Drug and Alcohol Dependence.* 32: 1993, pp. 231–237.

16. F.H. Gawin and H.D. Kleber, "Abstinence Symptomatology and Psychiatric Diagnosis in Cocaine Abusers." Archives of General Psychiatry. 43: 1986, pp. 107–113.

17. Ibid.

18. U.S. Department of Health and Human Services, Public Health Service Estimates from the Drug Abuse Warning Network. 1992 Estimates of Related Emergency Room Episodes, Advance Report Number, September 1993.

19. J. Maytal, S. Shinnar, S.L. Moshe, and L.A. Alvarez, "Low Morbidity Mortality of Status Eptilepticus in Children." *Pediatrics.* 83: 1989, pp. 323–331.

20. G.E. Billman and R.S. Hoskins, "Cocaine-induced Ventricular Fibrillation: Protection Offered By the Calcium-channel Antagonist Verapamil." *FASEB Journal.* 3: 1988, pp. 2990–2995.

21. N.S. Schwartzberg, "Cocaine Effect on Babies Questioned." *Newsday.* July 28, 1992. pp. 1, 55.

22. B.F. Grant and T.C. Hartford, "Concurrent and Simultaneous Use of Alcohol With Cocaine: Results of a National Survey." *Drug and Alcohol Dependence.* 25: 1990, pp. 97–104, .

23. T. Randall, "Cocaine, Alcohol Mix in Body to Form Even Longer Lasting, More Lethal Drug." *Journal of the American Medical Association.* 267: 1992, p. 1043.

24. S. Shelmutt, T.J. Hudzik, D.L. Lattin, and D.E. McMillan, "Effects of Cocaine and Ethylcocaine on Schedule-controlled Responding in Rats." *Pharmacology, Biochemistry and Behavior.* 43: 1992, pp. 509–511.

25. E.F. McCance-Katz, L. Price, C.J. McDougle, J.E. Kosten, and P.I. Jatlow, "Concurrent Cocaine-ethanol Ingestion in Humans: Pharmacology, Physiology, Behavior and the Role of Cocaethylene." *Psychopharmacology.* III: 1993, pp. 39–46.

26. P.J. Goldstein, H.H. Brownstein, P.J. Ryan, and P.A. Bellucci, "Most Drug-related Murders Result From Crack Sales, Not Use." *Drug Policy Letter.* March / April 1990, pp. 6–9.

Chapter 4

1. D. Franklin, "Hooked/Not Hooked: Why Isn't Everyone an Addict?" *Health.* November/December 1990, pp. 39–52.

2. "Coke Inc.: Inside the Big Business of Drugs." E. Goode, *Drugs, Society, and Behavior,* 93/94. Guilford, Conn.: The Dushkin Publishing Group, 1993, pp. 20–29.

3. Ibid.

4. L.N. Robins, "The Vietnam Drug User Returns." *Special Action Office for Drug Abuse Prevention Monograph* Series A. No. 2 May, 1974, Contract No. HSM-42 pp. 72-75.

5. D. Kandel and K. Yamaguchi, "From Beer to Crack: Developmental Patterns of Drug Involvement." *American Journal of Public Health.* 83: 1993, p. 851.

6. S. Rorner, "Up in Smoke: Why Do So Many Kids Ignore All the Evidence Condemning Cigarettes?" *The Washington Post National Weekly Edition.* December 1991, pp. 16–22.

7. U.S. Department of Education: "What Works: Schools Without Drugs." U.S. Government Printing Office: Washington, D.C., 1987. pamphlet.

8. R. Aniskiewicz and E. Wysong, "Evaluating DARE: Drug Education and the Multiple Meaning of Success." *Policy Studies Review.* 9: 1990, p. 727.

9. R.H. Blum, E. Blum, and E. Garfield, "Drug Education: Results and Recommendations." Lexington, Mass.: DC Heath, 1976.

10. B.A. Horger, P.J. Wellman, A. Morien, B.T. Davies, and S. Schenk, "Caffeine Exposure Sensitizes Rats to the Reinforcing Effects of Cocaine." *NeuroReport.* 2: 1991, pp. 53–56.

11. N.L. Benowitz, "Clinical Pharmacology and Toxicology of Cocaine." *Pharmacology & Toxicology.* 72: 1993, pp. 3–12.

12. R.D. Weiss, "Relapse to Cocaine Abuse After Initiating Desipramine Treatment." *Journal of the American Medical Association.* 260: 1988, pp. 2545–2546.

13. T.R. Kosten, M.I. Rosen, R. Shottenfeld, and D. Ziedonis, "Buprenorphine For Cocaine and Opiate Dependence." *Psychopharmacology Bulletin.* 28: 1992, pp. 15–20.

14. S.T. Higgins, A.J. Budney, W.K. Bickel, J.R. Hughes, F. Foerg and G. Badger, "Achieving Cocaine Abstinence with a Behavioral Approach." *American Journal of Psychiatry.* 150: 1993, pp. 763–769.

15. A.R. Childress, A.T. McLellan, R. Ehrman, and C.P. O'Brien, "Classically Conditioned Responses in Opioid and Cocaine Dependence: A Role in Relapse?" In: Ray, B.A. (Ed.) Learning factors in substance abuse. National Institute on Drug Abuse Research Monograph #84, U.S. Government Printing Office: Washington, D.C. pamphlet.

16. T.J. Crowley, "Doctor's Drug Abuse Reduced During Contingency Contracting Treatment." *Alcohol and Drug Research,* 6: pp. 299–307.

17. F.B. Glaser and A.C. Ogborne, "What We Would Most Like to Know: Does AA Really Work?" *British Journal of Addiction.* 77: 1982, p. 123.

Chapter 5

1. P.M. O'Malley, L.D. Johnston, and J.G. Bachman, "Quantitative and Qualitative Changes in Cocaine Use Among American High School Seniors, College Students, and Young Adults." *NIDA Research Monograph.* 110: 1991, pp. 19–43.

2. D. Franklin, "Hooked/Not Hooked: Why Isn't Everyone an Addict?" *Health.* November/December 1990, pp. 39–52.

3. This is a true story, but the name has been changed.

Chapter 6

1. G.E. Woody, H.C. Urschel III, and A. Alterman, "The Many Paths to Drug Dependence." Glantz, M. and Pickens, R. (Eds.). *Vulnerability to Drug Abuse.* American Psychological Association: Washington, D.C., 1992, pp. 491–507.

2. K.R. Merikangas, B.J. Rounsaville, and B.A. Prusoff, "Familial Factors in Vulnerability to Substance Abuse." Glantz, M. and Pickens, R. (Eds.). *Vulnerability to Drug Abuse.* American Psychological Association: Washington, D.C., 1992, pp. 75–97.

3. Ibid.

4. C. Holden, "Probing the Complex Genetics of Alcoholism." *Science.* January 11, 1991, pp. 163–164.

5. Alcohol and Health: Fifth special report to the U.S. Congress, DHHS Publication No. ADM 84 1291, U.S. Government Printing Office, Washington, D.C., 1984. pamphlet.

Further Reading

American Academy of Clinical Psychiatrists, "Cocaine Abuse and its Treatment," *The Journal of Clinical Psychiatry*, 49 (Supplement), 1988.

Benowitz, N.L. Clinical Pharmacology and Toxicology of Cocaine. *Pharmacology & Toxicology*, 72: 1993.

Cole, L. *Never Too Young To Die: The Death of Len Bias*. New York: Pantheon, 1989.

Gawin, F.H., and E.H. Ellinwood. "Cocaine and other Stimulants: Action, Abuse and Treatment." New England Journal of Medicine, 318: 1988.

Goode, E. Drugs, Society, and Behavior. Eighth edition, Guilford, CT: The Dushkin Publishing Group, Inc., 1993.

Johanson, C.E. *Cocaine: A New Epidemic*. New York: Main Line Book Co., 1992.

Johanson, C.E., and M.W. Fischman. "The Pharmacology of Cocaine Related to its Abuse." *Pharmacological Reviews*. 1989.

Peterson, R.C., and R.C. Stillman. Cocaine: NIDA Research Monograph #13. Washington, D.C. 20402. Stock number 017-024-00592, 4, 1977.

Ray, O., and C. Ksir. *Drugs, Society & Human Behavior*. Sixth edition. St. Louis: Mosby, 1993.

Rice-Licare, J., and K. Delaney-McLoghlin. Cocaine Solutions: Help for Cocaine Abusers and Their Families. Binghamton, NY: Haworth Press, 1990.

Rusche, S., and P. Kemp. You Have the Right to Know: Cocaine, a Drug Education Curriculum for Parents, Teachers and Young People. 2296 Henderson Mill Road, Suite 300, Atlanta, GA 30345, National Families in Action.

Shaffer, H.J., and S.B. Jones. Cocaine: The Struggle Against Impulse. Lexington, MA: Lexington Books, 1988.

Warner, E.A. "Cocaine Abuse." *Annals of Internal Medicine.* 119: 1993.

Williams, T. The Cocaine Kids: The Inside Story of a Teenage Drug Ring. Reading, MA: Addison-Wesley, 1989.

Index